THE SPIRIT

Christian Belief for Everyone series

Book 4

THE SPIRIT OF GRACE

Alister McGrath

First published in Great Britain in 2015

Society for Promoting Christian Knowledge
36 Causton Street
London SW1P 4ST
www.spckpublishing.co.uk

British Library Cataloguing-in-Publication Data
A catalogue record for this book is available from the British Library

ISBN 978–0–281–06839–5
eBook ISBN 978–0–281–06628–5

Typeset by Graphicraft Limited, Hong Kong
First printed in Great Britain by Ashford Colour Press
Subsequently digitally printed in Great Britain

eBook by Graphicraft Limited, Hong Kong

Produced on paper from sustainable forests

Contents

————◆◆◆————

v

Introduction

I was being interviewed on an American radio show about the importance of creeds. 'So why do we use creeds, then?' my host asked. I did what I always do on these occasions. I told him about the need to be able to summarize the key theme of our faith and make sure that we don't leave out anything that's really important. I asked my audience to imagine that they had been asked what Christians believe about God, and made the point that the creeds give us a checklist of things that we need to talk about. 'Like the Holy Spirit?' my host asked.

'Sure,' I replied.

'That's the bit I always prefer to leave out,' he told me. 'It's just too hard for me.'

I know what he meant. A lot of Christians feel that parts of the creed are obscure or difficult and steer clear of them, and many find the Holy Spirit especially difficult to manage. Some even go as far as to develop their own personal 'creeds', which are the bits of the real creeds that they especially like or feel that they can cope with. But one of the reasons the creeds are there is to challenge us to go beyond our personal comfort zones – to explore what the Church has believed down the ages, and not rest content with what we personally find attractive or manageable.

In the first three volumes of this series on the basic themes of the Christian creeds, we have looked at the nature of faith, the Christian understanding of God, and the identity and significance of Jesus of Nazareth. In this fourth volume, we move on to the next major set of beliefs presented, asking what the Apostles' Creed means when it speaks of 'the Holy Spirit, the holy catholic Church, the communion of saints, and the forgiveness of sins'.

These themes are reflected in the title of this volume – *The Spirit of Grace* – that reminds us, first of all, that God is active in the world. The creeds make it clear that the Holy Spirit brings life and renewal to believers and the Church. Second, the creeds affirm the graciousness of God, seen especially in the forgiveness of sins. And, finally, the creeds remind us of the importance of the Church as the community of faith. We will be exploring these three interconnected ideas in the following pages, and considering what impact they may have on how we live and think as Christians.

For many Christians, the Holy Spirit is one of the more puzzling aspects of both the creeds and the Christian faith. But as we saw earlier in *The Living God*, the rich Christian experience of God demands that we think of God as a living presence in the world and in our lives. The rise of the Charismatic movement in many parts of the Christian Church is a telling sign of the rediscovery of this aspect of the nature of God. Faith is not just about ideas; it is about a growing relationship with God, enabled by the Spirit. As William Temple (1881–1944), a former Archbishop of Canterbury, put it, 'Faith is not only the assent of our minds to doctrinal propositions: it is the commitment of our whole selves into the hands of a faithful Creator and merciful Redeemer.'[1]

Part of our journey of faith is exploring its landscape in greater detail. I often find it helpful to think of faith as embracing something that we know we don't fully grasp. We realize that we stand on the brink of something that is vast and deep, which needs to be explored and appreciated. That's why it's so important to talk about growing in faith. Christianity is indeed about salvation and redemption, in that God brings us to a place of safety and abides with us. It's like people fleeing from persecution arriving on a beautiful island that offers them safety. And as they settle into their new home, they begin to explore it and appreciate its richness and beauty. The creeds are an excellent basis for that journey of exploration, signposting the riches of faith that we need to discover and appreciate.

Up to this point, we have not really considered the Christian understanding of human nature, although we could perhaps have discussed this when we were thinking about the doctrine of creation. However, I feel it makes more sense to consider this concept in connection with the Holy Spirit. One important reason for taking this course is that it allows us to do justice to the theme of God 'breathing life' into humanity – not merely in creation, but throughout our lives. If we are to understand the important place of spirituality in the Christian faith, we need to grasp both the idea that humanity has been created in order to relate to God and the role of the Holy Spirit in enabling and sustaining that relationship. This naturally leads us on to the idea of grace, which many see as lying at the heart of the Christian faith. To say that God is gracious means that God acts for our good in a way that is undeserved: a way that reflects God's love and generosity rather than our achievements or status.

And so we come to the creeds' statements about the Church. Many Christians are perfectly happy to attend church, although they may have little understanding of it or its role in the Christian life. What, indeed, do we mean when we speak about 'the Church'? And how may we think of the Church as nourished and sustained by the Holy Spirit? The final two chapters of the book help us reflect on the role of the community of faith in nurturing individual believers' lives. I will map out some basic positions and issues to help you think this through. You will have to make up your own mind about which way of thinking about the Church seems best!

As before, I take great pleasure in being able to dedicate this book to the people of the Shill Valley and Broadshire benefice in the diocese of Oxford, consisting of the churches in the Cotswold villages of Alvescot, Black Bourton, Broadwell, Broughton Poggs, Filkins, Holwell, Kelmscott, Kencot, Langford, Little Faringdon, Shilton and Westwell. This book, like the others in this series, is based on sermons I have preached in those village churches.

Alister McGrath

1

The Holy Spirit: the giver of life

The eighteenth President of the United States, Ulysses S. Grant (1822–85), was of Scottish extraction, and perhaps it was inevitable that he would eventually visit Scotland to trace his family roots. While there, he was introduced to the game of golf. A local golfer set up a ball on a tee and – after due ceremony – took a whack with his club. When the turf had settled, everyone noticed that the ball was still there. The golfer had missed it. He tried again. Once more clods of grass flew into the air. The ball remained where it was. After watching several of these inept attempts, Grant confessed himself puzzled. Golf seemed to provide lots of exercise. But what exactly was the point of that little white ball?[1]

As every golfer is aware, that little white ball is of central importance, although the player does have to know what to do with it! In a similar way, some Christians, particularly those within Charismatic renewal movements, have no problems understanding the significance of the Holy Spirit, while to many others the idea is a bit of a puzzle and they're not sure quite what to make of it.

I hope this chapter will encourage a greater appreciation of the work of the Holy Spirit, the 'Lord and giver of life', as the creeds put it. God is able to breathe new life into our souls and the Church, rekindle our flagging faith and inflame our passion for God. But before we explore this great theme, it may be useful to remind ourselves about the sort of God that Christianity does not believe in (that we earlier touched on in *The Living God*): the famous 'divine watchmaker', popularized by the English writer William Paley in the nineteenth century.

An impoverished view of God: the divine watchmaker

William Paley (1743–1805) was an Anglican clergyman who appreciated the power of a good sermon illustration. Like so many preachers, he borrowed ideas from other people, and it was in a 1718 book by a Dutch writer that he found what was to become his trademark analogy of God as a watchmaker. Paley declared that God was like someone who had designed and constructed a complicated piece of machinery – like a clockwork watch. (Of course, no well-dressed Victorian gentleman would be seen in public without one.)

Why did William Paley think this was such a good sermon illustration? Because the watch showed evidence of having been designed. Every aspect, from its glass face to its cogwheels, signalled that it had been constructed for a specific purpose. Wasn't God just like a watchmaker? Looking at the complex structures of the world around us, can we not see the same evidence of design?

Now there's a lot in Paley's analogy. Some aspects of it are good, such as the recognition that the wonderful complexities of the natural world call out for an explanation, and that the Christian doctrine of creation provides one. But other aspects of the analogy are useless. What is remotely helpful about thinking of God as someone who makes a watch, winds it up and leaves it to tick? It's a very inadequate and ultimately non-Christian idea because it portrays a God who is disengaged with the created world and with us: someone who makes the world, sets it going – and then walks away, leaving it to its own devices. An absentee God who cares nothing for the created order is not one a Christian would recognize. Paley's model invites us to think of a creator God and no other kind. Now Christianity affirms that God is indeed the creator, as the creeds make perfectly clear. But there is very much more to God than this. Quite frankly, Paley's God is very dull and uninteresting.

The doctrine of the Trinity sets before us a rich, complex and wonderful vision of God, which makes Paley's deity seem miserably inadequate and uninteresting. For a start, the creeds insist that God actively chose to come into our world in order to redeem us. As we saw in *Lord and Saviour: Jesus of Nazareth*, God enters into our world and our history in the great act of salvation we call 'incarnation'. You may remember I quoted C. S. Lewis's rather apposite remark that God 'descended into his own universe, and rose again, bringing human nature up with him'.[2] Immediately, we realize that the God who Lewis is talking about is much more interesting than Paley's disengaged and absentee God. As Lewis realized, God *chose* to enter the world, and bring about our redemption. God cares for us – and acts to show that love.

But there is more to the Trinitarian vision of God than this. It declares that God is – and always has been – present and active in the world and in human lives, in and through the Holy Spirit. It is the nature and the role of the Holy Spirit that we will be considering in this chapter.

One of the more noticeable differences between the Apostles' Creed and the Nicene Creed is that the first simply affirms faith in the Holy Spirit, while the second offers a fuller, more substantial description of the importance of the Spirit in the Christian faith.

> We believe in the Holy Spirit, the Lord, the giver of life,
> who proceeds from the Father and the Son,
> who with the Father and the Son is worshipped and glorified,
> who has spoken through the prophets.[3]

There is a huge amount of wisdom distilled into these four lines. What does the Nicene Creed mean when it speaks of the Holy Spirit as the 'Lord and giver of life'? Let's begin by considering the witness to the Spirit in the Old Testament.

The Holy Spirit in the Old Testament: four leading themes

The English language uses at least three words – 'wind', 'breath' and 'spirit' – to translate the single Hebrew word *ruach*, but this important term has a depth of meaning virtually imposs-ible to reproduce in English. It is hardly surprising then that many of our versions of the Old Testament fail to convey the richness of the original image. If we want to fully under-stand the range of ideas associated with the idea of God as spirit, we need to tease out some of the themes expressed through this Hebrew word.

First, the Old Testament links the Holy Spirit with life, and especially with the giving or restoration of life. In creating Adam, God breathed into him the breath of life, as a result of which he became a living being (Genesis 2.7). The basic difference between someone who is alive and someone who is dead is that the first breathes and the second doesn't. In the old days, hospital doctors would often hold a mirror close to the mouth of someone who they believed had just died. If there was no breath condensing on the mirror, there was no life.

Life is about breathing! God is the one who breathes the breath of life into empty shells and makes them live. Just as God brought Adam to life, so God is able to bring individuals and his Church to life through his Spirit today. The famous vision of the valley of the dry bones (Ezekiel 37.1–14) also illustrates this point. The bones only come to life when breath enters into them (Ezekiel 37.9–10). God is the one who gives life, and the one who is able to bring the dead back to life.

Dorothy L. Sayers often wrote about how she struggled with that 'odd and difficult phrase' that describes the Holy Spirit as the 'Lord and giver of life'. Yet, in the end, she worked out what it was all about. Sayers was clear that a fulfilled human life was about more than mere physical existence. It was about living for a reason, with purpose and joy. That's what she came to find in this clause of the creed. 'The Christian affirms that the life in him proceeds from the eternal creativeness, and that therefore so far as he is moved by that creativeness, and so far only, he is truly alive.' Christianity is about coming to life – 'the right kind of life, the creative and godlike life'.[4]

The second theme associated with God as spirit is that of power, especially the power of the wind (remember, the Hebrew word *ruach* also has this meaning). We are all used to seeing things being moved by the invisible force of the wind, such as great sailing ships majestically crossing oceans, papers blowing across the road or trees bending in a gale. Old Testament writers saw an obvious parallel between the wind and the way in which God acted. God, like the wind, is an unseen force who acts upon the natural world and human beings.

A third approach to thinking about God as spirit (that, as we shall see, overlaps with the second) concerns the various ways in which God's activity is experienced. Sometimes God seems like a judge, one who breaks us down in order to humble us; at other times, God appears as one who refreshes us, like water in a dry land. Israel bordered the Mediterranean Sea on the west and the great deserts on the east. When the wind blew from the east, it brought a mist of fine sand that scorched vegetation and parched the earth. The western winds, however, brought rain as they blew in from the sea, and the intensity of the desert heat was mitigated by these gentle cooling breezes.

In short, Israel's experience of the wind was complex, and that pretty much mirrored her experience of God! At the time the prophet Isaiah was writing, Israel was held captive in Babylon. To many, it seemed as if the great Babylonian Empire was a permanent historical feature that nothing could remove. Yet the prophet proclaimed its decay and fall. God alone is permanent and all else is in a state of flux and change: 'The grass withers, the flower fades; but the word of our God will stand for ever' (Isaiah 40.8). The rise and fall of the Roman Empire, and more recently the British Empire, must remind us of this point, so powerfully developed through the model of God as the scorching desert wind.

God is also compared by the Old Testament writers to the rain brought by the western wind (Hosea 6.3), refreshing the land. What had been dry, arid and barren ground suddenly turned green, as all sorts of plant life seemed to appear from nowhere. We can think of ourselves as travellers through a dry land who suddenly discover an oasis. In the midst of our weariness and anxiety, God refreshes us.

And finally, Old Testament writers saw the Holy Spirit as the one who inspired prophecy. This important point is echoed in the creed's declaration that the Holy Spirit 'spoke through the prophets': that is, individuals who discerned God's purpose within history, having been temporarily endowed with the gift of the Holy Spirit.

All these ideas are developed further in the New Testament, as we shall now see.

The Holy Spirit in the New Testament: three leading themes

The New Testament builds on the Old Testament witness to the Holy Spirit, emphasizing that God is active both within the created order and within human existence. The life, death and resurrection of Jesus of Nazareth are clearly understood to mark a new phase in the presence and activity of the Spirit. The Old Testament spoke of the Spirit as a powerful wind blowing over the face of the waters, a shaping energy that gave life and direction to humanity. In the New Testament, this energy is understood to be focused on the person of Jesus.

Perhaps the most dramatic description of this development is found in Peter's famous speech, delivered on the day of Pentecost in Jerusalem (Acts 2.1–29). His argument is simple: the great Old Testament prophecy of God pouring out his Spirit on all humanity is now fulfilled, on account of Jesus of Nazareth. A new day – the 'Day of the Lord' – has dawned.

What does this mean? To find out, let's consider some of the roles of the Holy Spirit, as set out in the New Testament.

One of the most important of these is clearly the empowerment of believers. Just as the wind fills a boat's sails, so the Holy Spirit gives direction and movement to the life of faith. Without the Spirit, we become spiritually becalmed. As we have just seen, this idea is present in the Old Testament, but now it becomes clear that, far from being an impersonal force, the Spirit is in fact an intensely personal manifestation of the power of God. (For such reasons, many Christians feel uneasy about referring to the Holy Spirit as 'it'.) So in John's Gospel we find the Holy Spirit described as the 'comforter' or 'advocate', the one who consoles us, encourages us and stands by us in moments of doubt and despair. Another facet of this task, also mentioned in John's Gospel, is the way in which the Spirit brings to mind the words and deeds of Jesus of Nazareth. 'The Holy Spirit, whom the Father will send in my name, will teach you everything, and remind you of all that I have said to you' (John 14.26).

A second role of the Holy Spirit is that of 'illuminator'. How are we to make sense of the Bible and apply it to our lives? Many of the New Testament letters emphasize that we are not left on our own to wrestle with such questions: God somehow equips, enables or guides us throughout the journey of faith.

> I pray that the God of our Lord Jesus Christ, the Father of glory, may give you a spirit of wisdom and revelation as you come to know him, so that, with the eyes of your heart enlightened, you may know what is the hope to which he has called you, what are the riches of his glorious inheritance among the saints, and what is the immeasurable greatness of his power for us who believe. (Ephesians 1.17–19)

Most Christians would hold that the Spirit does not provide Christians with a new revelation of God, but rather with a deeper understanding of what has already been revealed, and a sense of how this might affect the way in which we live, or help us reach a decision about what we ought to do.

A third aspect of the work of the Spirit is dwelling within believers: 'Do you not know that you are God's temple and that God's Spirit dwells in you?' (1 Corinthians 3.16). The gift of the Holy Spirit is seen as a 'pledge' of our salvation, a 'seal' that confirms our relationship with God. Both of these ideas are borrowed from the commercial world of the first century, in which the New Testament letters were written.

For Paul, God has confirmed our salvation 'by putting his seal on us and giving us his Spirit in our hearts as a first instalment' (2 Corinthians 1.22). The Greek term *arrabōn*, usually translated as 'pledge' or 'first instalment', refers to a deposit paid in advance to secure the purchase of an item. Legally, the item now belongs to the buyer, who is under an obligation to pay the remainder of the price at an agreed time. The granting of the Holy Spirit is seen as a portion of the full riches of God to keep us going until we enter the New Jerusalem. God's greatest gift to us is not some commodity that bears no relation to him but, gloriously, the living presence of God in our hearts and souls.

The image of a seal refers to an imprint, often in wax, which proved the authenticity of a letter or document (such as a contract) in Roman times. The seal was a sign of trustworthiness, a reassurance that promises made would be honoured. In Chinese culture, the 'chop' still plays an important role. It is a personal seal, usually crafted from stone, which is dipped in red paste and stamped on documents or artwork as a mark of their authenticity. Like a signature on a cheque or other financial document, it denotes a pledge of commitment that will be fully honoured in the future.

We find this idea in John Calvin's definition of faith, which many regard as one of the most comprehensive and helpful to have been developed by a Christian theologian. Here is what he has to say:

> [Faith] is a steady and certain knowledge of the divine benevolence towards us, which is founded upon the truth of the gracious promise of God in Christ, and is both revealed to our minds and sealed in our hearts by the Holy Spirit.[5]

This richly Trinitarian understanding focuses on the 'gracious promises' of God, revealed and confirmed by the life, death and resurrection of Jesus of Nazareth, which the Holy Spirit plays a critical role in *appropriating* and *applying*. The Holy Spirit acts upon us, illuminating our minds and opening our hearts, so that we can receive and be transformed by the truths of faith.

One of the points that Calvin is able to make through this definition of faith is that the Christian faith is about more than simply believing that certain things are true. Christianity is not just about understanding; it is about renewal and transformation, through the power of a God whose trustworthiness is shown in and through Jesus of Nazareth. The Holy Spirit is understood as the agent of both illumination and transformation, opening us up to the truth and presence of the living God.

This theme of the Spirit as the one who enables us to trust God and grasp the promises made to us in Christ is of major importance to the devotional life of many Christians. It is, for example, an important aspect of a Christian understanding of prayer. 'The Spirit helps us in our weakness; for we do not know how to pray as we ought, but that very Spirit intercedes with sighs too deep for words' (Romans 8.26). Prayer is about being in the presence of God, laying out what is on our hearts.

Having sketched some themes from the Old and New Testaments, we need to explore more thoroughly how Christians have thought about the Holy Spirit and how this helps us on our own spiritual journey. Let's begin by thinking about the idea of the Spirit as the 'breath of God'.

The Spirit as the breath of God

I had gone camping with some fellow students. Being poor, like most students back in the early 1970s, we had decided to cycle along the Loire valley with the minimum of expense. We happily camped in hedgerows when we couldn't find proper campsites. One cold night, we lit a fire with our last match so we could cook our supper, and when the wood was burning, the three of us got things ready for the meal. Unfortunately, we forgot to appoint someone to look after the fire. It went out.

We stared at the dead fire, wondering what to do. All the shops were shut, so there was no chance of buying more matches. I was toying with the idea of rubbing two sticks together when one of my friends got down on his knees and began to blow softly on the embers. Ever so slowly, the embers began to glow. Then, as they got red, my friend blew harder and harder. Eventually the fire came back to life and we had a great hot supper. We probably enjoyed it all the more, knowing that we nearly didn't have one at all!

Let's stay with this image of breath bringing a dying fire back to life. It is widely used as an analogy for God's renewal of our faith in times of doubt, despair or helplessness. The famous hymn of Bianco da Siena (d. 1399) expresses this idea in words that have become familiar to many:

> Come down, O love divine,
> seek thou this soul of mine,
> and visit it with thine own ardour glowing;
> O Comforter, draw near,
> within my heart appear,
> and kindle it, thy holy flame bestowing.[6]

The Holy Spirit – here referred to as the 'Comforter' – is seen as an agent of renewal. The one who gave us life in the first place can give us new life when we are run down, exhausted and demoralized. The God who creates can also recreate.

Breath is both a sign and a source of life. When Christians talk about a 'living God', they are declaring that God lives and enables others to live. 'The spirit of God has made me, and the breath of the Almighty gives me life' (Job 33.4). In *The Living God*, we reflected on the Christian understanding of creation: when we speak about God creating humanity, we do not think in terms of being formed as empty lifeless shells or clockwork machines. God brings us to life, not in the sense of winding up a clockwork mechanism but by enabling us to exist.

Many of us have seen artificial respiration – the process by which someone breathes on behalf of someone who can no longer do this for him or herself. This 'mouth-to-mouth resuscitation' involves taking a deep breath of air and blowing into another person's lungs. The pressure of the air inflates the lungs, the oxygen in the air begins to circulate, and the patient can soon breathe without the need for further help.

But without intervention, the patient would die. He needs someone else to breathe for him until he is able to do it on his own. This familiar analogy is a good way of thinking about the Holy Spirit. God breathes into us, to make us alive and to keep us alive. It's not something that we can always manage on our own. We need help.

Let's tease out another theme that has been implicit in some of the ideas that we have been exploring. As we saw in *The Living God*, we have been created in order to relate to God. It's an insight that is beautifully expressed in the famous prayer of Augustine of Hippo (354–430): 'You have made us for yourself, and our heart is restless until it finds its rest in you.'[7] Notice that we have been created with the *capacity* to relate to God – it is a *possibility*, not something that is already part of our created nature. The God-shaped gap within us doesn't come with God already plugged in. Or, to use the New Testament's image, we are a temple within which the Holy Spirit may dwell. But the temple stands empty unless the Holy Spirit is present.

Perhaps the most discussed New Testament passage on this theme is the account of the night-time conversation between Jesus and Nicodemus (John 3.1–21). Nicodemus wants to know more about the teaching of Jesus of Nazareth, clearly sensing that this will take him to the heart of things. In responding, Jesus declares that 'no one can see the kingdom of God without being born from above' (John 3.3). The Greek word *anōthen*, here translated as 'from above', can also mean 'again'. A spiritual rebirth is needed, from above rather than below, through the Spirit rather than through water.

'No one can enter the kingdom of God without being born of water and Spirit' (John 3.5). We could think of the life of faith as a kind of supplementation of natural human existence, in which our lives are enriched and transformed through the presence of the Holy Spirit. Nicodemus is astonished at this suggestion. How, he asks, can he be reborn in this way? Is he meant to climb inside his mother's womb all over again?

He has rather missed the point. Being born into the world is one thing; becoming alive spiritually is another. Coming to faith is about recognizing and embracing the 'life of the Spirit', in which we begin to live and think and become what God wants us to be through God's help and presence. It's a matter of breaking free from the world of nature and discovering the world of grace.

In his letters, Paul makes much the same point by speaking of two quite different ways of living – a physical life 'according to the flesh' and the life of faith 'according to the Spirit'. Christians, Paul argues,

> walk not according to the flesh but according to the Spirit. For those who live according to the flesh set their minds on the things of the flesh, but those who live according to the Spirit set their minds on the things of the Spirit.
>
> (Romans 8.4–5)

It's not an easy idea to grasp. So let's approach it from another angle.

The renewal of the heart and mind

One evening over dinner at my Oxford college back in the 1970s, I fell into conversation with an Irish doctor who had worked in a clinic in East Africa just after the Second World War. Conditions were very basic and the medics had only a limited stock of drugs at their disposal. Perhaps as a result of coming into contact with infected patients, he developed a fever. He became confused, found it impossible to walk and couldn't think straight. His colleagues did their best to relieve his symptoms but they couldn't cure the fever. After an anxious few days, fortunately it passed, and in due course he was able to return to work.

The memory of his close brush with death had clearly made a deep impression on the doctor, and led him to think hard about what to do with the rest of his life. But that wasn't the aspect of our conversation that I remember best. My new friend was musing about the impact of his infection: normally an athletic man, he found he couldn't even get out of his bed; normally a quick-thinking person, he had become confused and unable to string thoughts together; normally a very fluent and eloquent speaker, he could now only whisper and groan. Wouldn't it be wonderful, he remarked, if there was some kind of 'good infection' that would make us more energetic, intelligent and articulate – that would have the opposite effect on us to the one he had picked up!

It was an interesting thought, and one that remained with me. I had just been reading C. S. Lewis's chapter on 'Good infection' in *Mere Christianity*,[8] in which he develops a distinction between physical and spiritual existence. Lewis here uses two Greek words for life: *Bios*, which he takes to refer to the fact that we are alive in the sense that a plant or animal is alive, and *Zoe*, which he understands as the purposeful, meaningful life that God intends for us.

> We are not begotten by God, we are only made by Him: in our natural state we are not sons of God, only (so to speak) statues. We have not got *Zoe* or spiritual life: only *Bios* or biological life which is presently going to run down and die. Now the whole offer which Christianity makes is this: that

we can, if we let God have His way, come to share in the life of Christ . . . If we share in this kind of life we also shall be sons of God. We shall love the Father as [Christ] does and the Holy Ghost will arise in us. He came to this world and became a man in order to spread to other men the kind of life He has – by what I call 'good infection'.[9]

Lewis's imagery is that of us becoming 'infected' – but in a good way. To use his means of expressing himself, we stop being 'statues' and become 'sons of God'. We cease being empty shells, created by God, and instead become what God really wants us to be – people who have been reborn, renewed and transformed by God. We cease being empty temples, constructed by God, and instead become inhabited by God who dwells within the temple of our souls. The Holy Spirit – God inhabiting us – is then able to begin the work of transformation within us, renewing our minds and hearts.

As Lewis rightly saw, we are not merely told to become more like Jesus of Nazareth, as if the Christian faith were a set of orders barked at us by some distant and uncaring general; we are enabled to become so, by a God who enriches and graces our lives, redirects our wills and inspires us to do good. 'God has sent the Spirit of his Son into our hearts, crying, "Abba! Father!"' (Galatians 4.6), thus enabling us to pray and shaping us in the likeness of Jesus.

This has a major implication for Christian spirituality. The life of faith is not about a forced acquiescence to do God's will but a renewed – and, as a result, natural – instinct to want to do what matters to God. The Holy Spirit is seen as an agent of transformation, renewing our hearts, minds and wills so that we gradually come to love what God loves. Christians see this as the fulfilment of the great Old Testament prophecy in which God establishes a new covenant with Israel. No longer will the law be something external, written on tablets of stone. 'I will put my law within them, and I will write it on their hearts' (Jeremiah 31.33).

Understanding, experience and the Holy Spirit

As I mentioned in the Preface, Christians tend to be divided in their approaches to the Holy Spirit. Some, especially those within the Charismatic and Pentecostal movements, welcome an emphasis on Christian experience – one also found in early Methodism, with its stress on a 'living faith' experienced by the heart and not merely understood by reason. Charles Wesley's words from one of his best-known hymns witness to this way of perceiving the presence of the Holy Spirit:

> Still the small inward voice I hear,
> That whispers all my sins forgiven . . .
> I feel the life His wounds impart;
> I feel the Saviour in my heart.[10]

An emphasis on the experience of the Spirit can be argued to represent a welcome move away from very bookish or intellectual ways of thinking about the Christian faith. Why should those who cannot read, or who find abstract reasoning difficult, be disadvantaged in matters of faith? The Holy Spirit is the great leveller, making the rich experience of the living God available to all.

But not everyone feels so positively about experiential approaches to faith. Dorothy L. Sayers wrote to C. S. Lewis on 5 August 1946, making clear they made no sense to her. 'All spiritual experience is a closed book to me; in that respect I have been tone-deaf from birth.'[11] Sayers relied on reason and imagination to generate and sustain her faith, and saw no cause to appeal to the vagueness of religious experience to express or defend it. Others are wary of a 'touchy-feely' faith, which they consider may open them to the charge of emotionalism or subjectivism – that is, making what they feel the basis of what they believe.

Most readers will have little difficulty in sympathizing with these varying positions. They're not mutually exclusive. In fact, many would say that they can be woven together to give a richer and deeper vision of the Christian life.

Divergence within Christianity really reflects a strength. It is a classic theme of Christian spirituality that God deals with individuals according to their varying gifts and needs, humbling the arrogant on the one hand and encouraging the down-hearted on the other. The rationality of the Christian faith appeals to those who use their reason to seek for structures and meaning within the world, while its core theme of an active and present God connects up with those who are looking for stability and empowerment.

There is only one Holy Spirit, but our experience and appreciation of that Spirit differs and reflects our individual identity. We are not forced into a template! Each of us is special, with something unique to offer God, who takes the threads of our lives and weaves them into a greater pattern.

As this chapter draws to a close, it may be helpful to present a summary of some of the leading themes of the Christian understanding of the work of the Spirit.

The work of the Holy Spirit: an overview

What does the Holy Spirit do? Many theologians have tried to provide a summary of the work of the Spirit, and a good example is found in Basil of Caesarea's succinct statement:

> Through the Holy Spirit we are restored to paradise, led back to the Kingdom of heaven, adopted as children, given confidence to call God 'Father' and to share in Christ's grace, called children of light, and given a share in eternal glory.

The Christian tradition has generally understood the work of the Holy Spirit to focus on three broad areas: revelation, salvation and the Christian life. Let's look at each of these briefly.

Revealing God to us

The Holy Spirit helps make God known to us. The second-century theologian Irenaeus of Lyons wrote of the 'Holy Spirit, through whom the prophets prophesied, and our forebears learned of God and the righteous were led in the paths of justice'. The task of the Holy Spirit is to lead the faithful into God's truth; without that Spirit, truth remains elusive.

This idea is developed further in the notion of the 'inspiration of Scripture', which affirms that the Bible has a God-given authority. This doctrine, in various forms, is the common tradition of Christianity and has its origins in the Bible itself, most notably the affirmation that 'all Scripture is inspired by God' (2 Timothy 3.16). Most Christian theologians affirm the activity of the Holy Spirit both in the inspiration of Scripture and in the subsequent responsibility of the Church to interpret and apply this text.

Yet it is not simply God's revelation that is linked with the work of the Spirit; the Spirit is also widely regarded as being involved in the human response to that revelation.

Most Christian theologians have regarded faith itself as the result of the work of the Holy Spirit. For example, John Calvin highlighted the pivotal role of the Spirit in revealing God's truth and applying or 'sealing' this truth to humanity, to refer back to the quote on p. 10.

The appropriation of salvation

Christian theologians have noted how the Holy Spirit plays a critical role in illuminating, healing and enabling humanity to take hold of Christ, and thus benefit from his identity and his work. For example, the Second Vatican Council (1962–5) emphasized the role of the Spirit in preparing the human mind and heart for revelation and salvation:

> To make this act of faith, the grace of God and the interior help of the Holy Spirit must precede and assist, moving the heart and turning it to God, opening the eyes of the mind and giving joy and ease to everyone in assenting to the truth and believing it.

The energization of the Christian life

The importance of the role of the Spirit in relation to Christian prayer, spirituality and worship has been stressed by many writers, classic and modern. The fifth-century writer Cyril of Alexandria is one of many to emphasize the role of the Spirit in bringing unity within the Church. The Spirit is also important in relation to mission, as the *Catechism of the Catholic Church* (1994) notes:

> The Spirit prepares people, and goes out to them with his grace, in order to draw them to Christ. The Spirit manifests the risen Lord to them, recalls his word to them and opens their minds to the understanding of his Death and Resurrection.[12]

The Holy Spirit is thus integral to a Christian understanding of human nature and activity. We are brought to life, and empowered to act, by this Spirit. This points to the need for us to reflect further on what we understand by humanity. In the next chapter, we shall open up some of the themes of a Christian understanding of human nature and consider their implications for Christian life and thought.

2

Humanity: the climax of God's Creation

—•◦•—

Dorothy L. Sayers had a great gift for putting her finger on things that really matter. In a lecture of 1940, she reminded her audience that the creed 'purports to tell us the essential facts, not only about God, but about the true nature of man'.[1] So what are human beings? What makes us different from the rest of Creation, according to the Christian faith? It's one of the most important questions we can ask. The greatest ethical, social and political debates all depend on an understanding of what it means to be human, and on how our humanity may be expressed and fulfilled.

For example, consider the question of justice – a passionate concern for many in today's complex and broken world. Yet justice is not something that we can 'read off' the world. Indeed, some attempts to ground justice in nature have ended up promoting the Darwinian idea of the 'survival of the fittest'. But what of widows and orphans? Or the powerless and weak? In his penetrating and highly acclaimed writings on the nature of justice, Michael Sandel, who is Professor of Government at Harvard University, argues that any notion of justice depends upon beliefs about human nature, values and purpose.[2] Secular liberalism represents a hollow and shallow view of the world, which ends up merely defending the right of citizens to do whatever they please, as long as they hurt no one else. But real justice is about principles and ideals – about what human nature is and ought to be.

As we are beginning to see, a central theme of the Christian faith is that the Holy Spirit is the agent by which God enables things – including human beings – to become what they are meant to be. The Holy Spirit is the bringer of life and renewal. The creeds help us to realize that, without God, we have not really begun to live.

So what do the creeds tell us about human nature? What difference do these ideas make to us, and how do they connect up with the Holy Spirit?

On being human

'We are all nothing but atoms and molecules!' This was the punch-line to an atheist speaker's rather dreary lecture in London that I attended a few years ago. Human beings are insignificant, he declared. We need to get used to the idea that life is meaningless and pointless. The speaker invited his audience to abandon their delusions about themselves and make the bold and brave admission that we are the accidental product of a random process. Sure, it was hard to admit this. But that was why atheism was so cool! Better to be right than deluded.

He lost the audience's sympathy completely. As one bemused student remarked to me afterwards, that kind of atheism offered such a dull, bleak view of humanity that he couldn't imagine anyone taking it seriously. Even if it was right (which he very much doubted), it was so unimaginably drab that he suspected many would end up becoming religious just to get away from the sheer tedium of the speaker's godless world.

I agreed with him. But I also pointed out that the speaker was demonstrably wrong in his views about human nature. Why? Let me explain.

It's true that human beings are made up of atoms and molecules, that we are a walking collection of chemicals. If my quick calculation is right, human beings could be reduced to enough water to have a shower and enough fat to make half a dozen bars of soap. Those things would not raise any significant sum, so in one way the atheist speaker was right. But only in one way – and a very misleading way at that, as we'll discuss in a moment.

This process of reducing human beings to the function and value of commodities is called 'dehumanization'. It's what the Nazis did to those in the death camps, like Auschwitz. When people arrived in the camps, they were given numbers. No longer did they have names – chosen by loving and caring parents and often linking them with their family's history – they were now to be identified merely by a collection of digits. Then they were set to work, like impersonal cogs in a vast industrial machine. Their value was determined by what they could produce. And when they were no longer productive, they were killed. Their hair was used to stuff mattresses, and their gold fillings used to make bullion bars. They had ceased to be people and had become commodities. They had been dehumanized.

This reductionist view of humanity is set out in one of the less perceptive statements of the biologist and Nobel laureate Francis Crick:

> You, your joys and your sorrows, your memories and your ambitions, your sense of personal identity and free will, are in fact no more than the behaviour of a vast assembly of nerve cells and their associated molecules.[3]

C. S. Lewis regularly protested against reductionist accounts of reality. In *The Voyage of the Dawn Treader*, one of the children shows off his scientific knowledge of astronomy to Ramandu, an old man who lived on a Narnian island. 'In our world,' said Eustace, 'a star is a huge ball of flaming gas.' The old man was not impressed. 'Even in your world, my son, that is not what a star is, but only what it is made of.' Lewis's point was that we too easily fall into the trap of believing that describing what something is made of tells us what it really is.

The truth is that human beings can be defined at multiple levels, and each level helps us understand the complexity of human nature. The physicist will tell us that we are made of atoms and molecules. She's right. But she's wrong if she adds that ridiculous word 'just'. The chemist will tell us that life is the result of complex chemical reactions, leading to food being converted to energy. The physiologist will tell us about the various organs that make up the human body and what each of them does. But we transcend all of these levels of description! If humanity is defined by anything, it is not what we find at the bottom of the ladder, but at the top.

Richard Dawkins, the world's most prominent atheist, is interesting on this point. Dawkins was one of the high-profile defenders of the 'gene's eye' view of life, which was very popular back in the 1980s. For Dawkins, everything was determined by our DNA – the complex biological model that transmits genetic information. We are simply there to allow our genes to transfer themselves to future generations. These genes 'are in you and me; they created us, body and mind; and their preservation is the ultimate rationale for our existence'. Whether we like it or not, we exist simply in order to pass on our genes.[4]

Does that seem inadequate? Dawkins tells us that this is the way things are and we need to get used to it. 'DNA neither cares nor knows. DNA just is. And we dance to its music.' Viewed through the lens of Dawkins' aggressive scientific reductionism, all existence is nothing more than assemblies of molecules, some of which happened to be arranged in the form of those gene-perpetuating machines that we call 'human beings'. Yet there is a very telling passage at the end of his book *The Selfish Gene*, which many believe contradicts the whole analysis that precedes it. Having consistently argued that we are the prisoners of our genes, Dawkins makes the dramatic statement that there is something different about human beings! 'We, alone on earth, can rebel against the tyranny of the selfish replicators.' There is more to us than our biology. We are, Dawkins declares, able to transcend these limits!

Now in many ways Dawkins has simply evaded a problem of his own making. Having fallen into the trap of what many would see as a crude genetic determinism, he protests against its inadequacies. Yet his protest against the view that we are 'just' genes, or that our identity and character are determined by our DNA, is a recognition that there is more to human nature than a purely biological, chemical or physical account. Science helps us understand how we *function*; but there's a lot more to human identity than this.

What more needs to be said? The Christian view does not deny that we are made of atoms and molecules, nor that DNA exists and plays an important role in the transmission of genetic information. It does not seek to take away, but to add. It agrees that atoms, molecules and genes are all part of who we are, while insisting that we accept that there is more to human nature than this. It argues that we transcend the building blocks from which we are made, rather like an artistic masterpiece transcends its brush strokes.

Let's try to make this important point clearer. When I was young, my father and I visited some elderly sisters who lived close to us. My father wanted to make sure that they were coping with a viciously cold winter and see if they needed anything. While we were there, they showed us some of their prize possessions. Most of these were uninteresting to me – except for one. It was a personal hand-written letter from Winston Churchill, dating back to the 1950s, wishing them both a joyful Christmas and apologizing for not having seen them for so many years. Neither my father nor I had realized that these sisters were related to Churchill. They were clearly delighted with this letter, partly because it showed that they were connected to someone important, and partly because it was a genuinely interesting letter.

Now, in one sense, that letter was simply a piece of paper with some ink on it. To use that tired old phrase, so hope-lessly over-worked by atheist dogmatists, it was 'nothing but atoms and molecules'. But that is clearly a totally inadequate description of the letter. Yes, it was 'atoms and molecules'. But it was so much more than that. It was proof that these sisters were related to Winston Churchill. It was a token of his affection and concern.

The Genesis creation accounts emphasize that we are more than physical structures; the Spirit of God inhabits us. 'The LORD God formed man from the dust of the ground, and breathed into his nostrils the breath of life; and the man became a living being' (Genesis 2.7). Yes, we do originate from the dust; yes, we are formed of the material of the world around us; but we are more than this! Let's now begin to unpack how the Christian faith provides for an understanding of human nature.

The image of God

As we saw in *The Living God* (72–6), the Christian faith declares that human beings bear the 'image of God'. This helps us appreciate our accountability towards God, and the ability of the human mind to make some sort of sense of the world around us. But perhaps most importantly, it enables us to relate to God as we relate to those closest to us, whether friends or family. Companionship with God is what we are made for – God is both the source and the goal of human existence – and without God, we will never achieve our deepest aims, find our heart's desire or secure ultimate fulfilment.

One of the pithiest statements of this point is found in the *Westminster Shorter Catechism* (1647–8), which sets out 107 questions about faith, followed by snappy answers.

> Q. *What is the chief end of man?*
> A. Man's chief end is to glorify God, and to enjoy him for ever.

C. S. Lewis greatly admired this line of what he called the 'Scotch Catechism'. Why? Because 'in commanding us to glorify Him, God is inviting us to enjoy Him'. This is a wonderful summary of what the Christian faith tells us lies at the heart of human existence.

As we noted earlier, everyone has their own ideas about the true nature and goals of human nature. Secular humanism, for example, holds that human beings only achieve their true identity and meaning by rejecting religion and belief in God. Christians, on the other hand, believe that we find our true significance and destiny by embracing God. That's why so many Christians argue that Christianity is the real and best form of humanism. That may seem strange to some readers, so let me explain.

The word 'humanism' came into being at the time of the Renaissance and has nothing to do with secularism or atheism.[5] The term was hijacked in the last century by those arguing that humanity needs to be liberated from an oppressive belief in God. Yet the great humanists of the Renaissance – such as Erasmus of Rotterdam (1466–1536) – believed that God enriched and fulfilled human life and experience. To become what we are meant to be and to have the joy and peace that we are meant to have means embracing, loving and walking with God. Erasmus would be appalled at the dogmatic atheism that is now associated with the word 'humanism'!

Let's think more about this core Christian idea of God as our true goal. Some friends of my parents moved house a few years ago. Their new home was only half an hour's drive from the old one, and shortly after their arrival their cat went missing. After a while they gave up looking for him, assuming he had got lost. Some weeks later, they had a phone call from the new owners of their old house. Had they lost a cat? One had turned up at their home and was behaving as if it lived there. My parents' friends drove over immediately and were delighted to find their cat alive and well. The cat didn't seem so interested in them, however. It was the house he liked. And in the end, there he stayed. The new owners had by then become so fond of him that they adopted him.

The cat had a homing instinct. And so do we. We possess a built-in longing for God. And it remains a part of us, no matter how hard we try to suppress it, ignore it or explain it away as an irrational outcome of our evolutionary past.

Eternity has been planted in our hearts. I've always liked the poems of Francis Quarles (1592–1644), especially his *Emblems*, in which he compares the human soul to a magnetic needle, constantly attracted to the north pole of God:

> Like to the Artick needle, that does guide
> the wandering shade by his Magneticke pow'r.[6]

It's a nice image, which Quarles develops further by suggesting that God is like a 'lodestone' – a naturally magnetized piece of stone that draws metals (including compass needles) to itself. We are made in such a way that we are drawn to God, so that we can find our road home.

God established a relationship with humanity through creation, restored it through redemption and will bring it to completion in heaven. This idea is especially important as we begin to think about a theme that puzzles many – the idea of the 'soul'.

What is the soul?

One of my problems with Christianity as a young man was the idea that human beings consist of a mortal body and an immortal soul. I imagined the body as some kind of home for the latter, and that once you died, the soul went to heaven. I'm not sure where I got these ideas from or why I thought that they were an essential part of the Christian package. After all, there's no mention of them in the creeds.

When I became a scientist, I could see no reason whatsoever for believing in some immaterial and eternal soul, which was temporarily resident in the human body until death and then made its way somewhere else. If this was intrinsic to Christian belief, I had a bit of a problem.

Now some Christians do indeed believe in an immortal soul, like the great scholastic theologian Thomas Aquinas (1225–74). In the Middle Ages, a distinction was made between the 'body' and the 'soul' (Latin: *anima*). Humans, it was argued, were distinguished from all other animals and inanimate objects by the possession of a 'soul'. This approach was justified on biblical grounds, in that the New Testament generally speaks of 'body and soul', and occasionally of 'body, soul and spirit'. References to the 'body' were generally understood by medieval writers like Aquinas to refer to the physical and material parts of humanity, whereas the 'soul' was understood as an immaterial and eternal spiritual entity that merely resided within the human body.

But is this really how we ought to interpret the biblical statements about human identity? Many scholars in the twentieth century pointed out that the notion of an immaterial soul was a secular Greek concept rather than a biblical one. The vision of humanity found in the Old Testament was that of a single entity, an inseparable 'psychosomatic unit', with many facets or aspects. The Old Testament conceives of humanity 'as an animated body and not as an incarnate soul' (H. Wheeler Robinson).[7]

'Soul' is an Anglo-Saxon word used to translate a variety of biblical terms, many of which have the general sense of 'the basis of life' or 'a living being'. The Old Testament tends not to use these terms to refer to parts of the human body, but rather understands them as aspects of human existence. We see a similar trend in the New Testament. When Paul talks about not living or walking 'according to the flesh but according to the Spirit' (Romans 8.4), he isn't referring to two different parts of humanity – flesh and spirit. Rather, he is talking about two quite different ways of living: existing at a purely human level, and coming to life in a way that connects up with God.

We could thus think of the 'soul' as that aspect of our being that relates to God, or our God-given ability to enter into a relationship with God. This is what gives us our true identity in the first place, and maintains it in the second.

Why is this so important? For two reasons: first, because of how our identity is expressed, and second, because of how it is sustained. In our increasingly bureaucratic culture, most of us are identified through nationality, passport number, fingerprints or DNA. These are often highly efficient ways of distinguishing us from other people. For example, the chance of two people, including twins, having the same fingerprint is less than one in a billion.

Both fingerprints and DNA are coded mathematically to enable easy identification, especially in forensic contexts.[8] They are expressing our personal identity in a highly impersonal way. The issue here is that we would never normally define ourselves thus: we would more naturally think in terms of the things that we do and the people that matter to us.

It is a fact that our Christian identity is expressed by a name – not a number or code. 'Do not fear, for I have redeemed you; I have called you by name, you are mine' (Isaiah 43.1). Names express our uniqueness and value. To call someone by name is to demonstrate that you know her; she matters enough for you to remember what her name is.

Some of the farmers I know in the Cotswolds raise livestock for a living. Even though they often become very fond of the animals on their farms, they tell me they never give them names. Why not? Because it makes sending the animals to market very traumatic. As one farmer said to me, 'When you give an animal a name, it becomes special to you.'

Our identity is expressed within a network of relationships in which we both *belong* and *matter*, whether as a member of a family, as a friend or as a colleague. Christianity supplements this with one additional relationship – with the living God. Paul speaks in one of his letters of believers being 'adopted as his children' (Ephesians 1.5). This powerful image suggests someone who does not belong anywhere, or matter to anyone, being drawn into a new family and given a new identity and a new status because he or she is *wanted*; because he or she *matters*. In the ancient world, family identity was of crucial importance to an individual's sense of self-worth. Paul's point is that believers are members of God's family and as such have a new status and relationship. We shall consider this further in the next chapter.

This identity cannot be taken away from us. Someone may lose her job and with it the prestige and connections it brings. Someone may lose his memory and with it access to the past. But our relationship with God abides, and can never be erased or destroyed. It is nourished and sustained by the presence of the Spirit within us, who constantly reassures us that we are loved. 'When we cry, "Abba! Father!" it is that very Spirit bearing witness with our spirit that we are children of God, and if children, then heirs, heirs of God and joint heirs with Christ' (Romans 8.15–17).

Free and finite? The human dilemma

In the previous section, we emphasized the importance of our capacity to relate to God. We need to explore this a little further and ask what it tells us about the abilities and limitations of being human. The Christian tradition uses a significant range of terms to describe the relationship between the believer and God – love, faithfulness and commitment – ideas that are reflected and embedded in the best human relationships.

Some atheist writers, of course, would suggest that we have simply invented God and imposed values we respect, or desire to have ourselves, upon this imaginary relationship. But as we have seen, the Christian doctrine of creation provides us with a framework for declaring that the best in human life echoes our origins in God. Our values, ideas and actions may be seen as the afterglow of the act of creation, clarified and infused with passion in the life of Jesus of Nazareth.

One of the core themes of this understanding of creation is that a loving God creates a people capable of love – of loving one another and of loving God. This relationship exists at both the corporate level (the 'people of God') and the individual. God *offers* love to us, *gives* love to us and *invites* a response of love from us. 'God's love has been poured into our hearts through the Holy Spirit that has been given to us' (Romans 5.5). A number of points emerge from this.

First, although God is indeed love, God shows that love in and through Jesus of Nazareth. Actions speak louder than words, and God's demonstration of love confirms and extends what has been promised. Second, it takes two to be in a loving relationship. God may indeed love us, but unless we love God in return, no relationship has been established. We see here the idea of reciprocation, which is such an important aspect of the Christian understanding of a personal God.

Our interest in this section will actually focus on a third aspect of love. Love is something that must be freely accepted. An imposed love is no love at all. God has created us with the capacity to love and to respond to love. And in each case, love is an expression of freedom, in which we make ourselves vulnerable, open to rejection by the object of our love.

The theme of God's love being rejected by Israel is common in the prophetic writings, and is found in a particularly pointed form in some texts that many Christian churches appoint to be read during Lent, especially Passiontide. Why? Because the same pattern of spurned love is found in the betrayal, trial and crucifixion of Jesus of Nazareth.

What does all this point to? Simply that God created us with the freedom to say 'no'. The Old Testament prophets sometimes compare God to a parent who brought a child into the world. Having cared for the child, God watched with sadness as it went its own way, making mistakes and spurning its parent's love. Yet God waited for the child to return, as patiently and lovingly as the father of the prodigal watched from the roof of his house, hoping to see the return of his wayward son from the distant land where he was exiled (Luke 15).

So what sort of freedom do we have? At first sight, this seems a very easy question to answer. Both the Ten Commandments and the Sermon on the Mount tell us to choose to do good and to cease doing evil. Surely we can manage this?

Some within the Christian tradition have argued that this is the case, maintaining that Christians have an obligation to fulfil these commandments in their totality. Many others have been less sure. What if human nature is so weak and fallible that we turn out to be incapable of doing these things? The great Roman poet Ovid had little doubt about his own powerlessness. 'I see and approve better things, but follow the worse.'

Recognizing there is a problem here, we may put it down to a lack of moral fibre. Some like to think of addressing this deficiency in athletic terms: these things are too hard for us at present, but training and practice will make them achievable; maybe we can't break the record for the high jump or 100 metres sprint at the moment, but if we keep on trying we'll gradually become good enough to make the grade. Some prefer an educational model: we need to be taught how to be good, in much the same way as we are taught how to use a piece of software. Once we've mastered the technique, we'll be fine.

This is a nice idea, and one that captured the imaginations of many in Western Europe in the eighteenth century. The 'Age of Reason' argued that reason and science liberated people from bondage to outmoded superstitions. And having broken free from the bonds of religion and other irrational ideas, humanity could set out on the upward path to enlightenment and moral perfection. Reason and science would put an end to conflict and social tension.

Of course, it didn't work out like that. Our forebears might have been great at aspiring to social justice and world peace, but the massively destructive Great War of 1914–18 put an end to this dream, exposing it as a sad and unsustainable delusion. The Enlightenment told us that war was caused by religion, and by giving up on religion, the world would become a safer place. Yet historians are agreed that religion played virtually no role in causing the Great War. Nationalism, pride, greed and utter stupidity were all major contributing causes to this devastating war. But not religion.

This leads us on to consider a darker possibility: is there something in human nature that inclines us to do evil, even when we pay lip-service to the good? That steers us to do things we know we shouldn't do, or to fail to do the things we know we should? Much secular thinking about ethics is based on the assumption that we naturally want to do the right thing. But what if there is some fatal flaw within human nature that inclines us to do what suits our own agendas, when we know perfectly well that we ought to be doing something else?

In Christian theology, this flaw within human nature is called sin. In the remainder of this chapter, we will explore this theme in some detail.

The flaw within humanity: thinking about sin

The Christian faith has a rich notion of sin that it will probably be more helpful to describe than to define. In modern Western culture, some people find the idea of sin offensive, not because it is irrational (which it is not) but because it challenges the myth on which much of our culture has been constructed – that humanity is intrinsically good, and that it can achieve good unaided, without reference to God.

The 'New Atheism', well aware that the world is a mess, has an easy explanation for this state of affairs. The contradictions and failures of recent human history – that include the awkward arrival of the brutal totalitarian regimes of Nazism and Stalinism, not to mention weapons of mass destruction – are put down, somewhat implausibly, to the resurgence of religion. Yet both Lenin and Stalin saw the elimination of religion as one of their core objectives, so that they could create an atheist state.

There's a real problem here for the New Atheism. First, it has to confront the very awkward fact that Marxism–Leninism, the atheist ideology on which the Soviet Union was founded, failed to persuade Russians that atheism was intellectually or existentially preferable to Christianity. In the end, Stalin had to resort to force to eliminate religion. The New Atheism, which is wedded to the idea that religion generates violence, thus has to come to terms with the atheist use of violence to enforce its unpopular ideas.[9]

Yet, more importantly, we need to recall what happened following the collapse of the Soviet Union during the 1990s. Christopher Hitchens seems to think that the Russian people were delighted to be liberated from religion and rejoiced in the new rationalist paradise of the Soviet Union. Yet the moment this unpopular state collapsed, religion rebounded. People were free once more to believe in God! It doesn't fit the neat little slogans of the New Atheism, but it fits perfectly with the idea that we have a homing instinct for God that survives both repression and suppression.

Anyway, is human nature really as simple as these armchair philosophers suggest? Surely history shows up humanity's failures and weaknesses, pointing to some inbuilt flaw in human nature? The real problem for secular rationalists is that, having made human beings the 'measure of all things' (Protagoras), they somehow have to account for the shocking brutality we have seen in recent decades, including mass genocides. If there is no god, the blame for this brutality lies firmly and squarely with humanity – the same humanity that these people believe is fundamentally good and rational. This issue regularly emerges as a topic of concern in historical studies of the First World War. How on earth did intelligent people in the world's most advanced nations end up plunging into a massively destructive war, which nobody really won? The sheer senselessness and futility of war between highly industrialized nations had been demonstrated by Norman Angell in his pre-war bestseller *The Great Illusion*.[10] Angell made an excellent case, but these nations still ended up going to war in what many historians now regard as a moment of collective irrationality.

Christianity is characterized by a profoundly realistic view of human nature and uses the word 'sin' to describe the flaws in human nature. Although the word is often rather simplistically defined in purely moral terms, as if the essence of sin was behaving badly, the truth is that sin is a deep-rooted malaise within us – something that's built into our human identity. A Christian understanding of human nature avoids the fatalist belief that we can do nothing and the utopian delusion that we can do anything. Does this devalue human nature? Not in the least. It's just being honest about the way things are.

Blaise Pascal spoke of the 'grandeur and misery' of human nature. On the one hand, we are inspired by our vision of goodness which draws us upwards; on the other, we find ourselves dragged down into the mud by our selfishness and foolishness. It is a familiar dilemma, famously articulated by Paul: 'I do not do the good I want, but the evil I do not want is what I do' (Romans 7.19). Christian theology gives us a critical lens through which to view the complex motivations and mixed agendas of human beings. We bear God's image, yet we are sinful. We are capable of good, but we are also capable of evil.

G. K. Chesterton was one of many to suggest that the Christian idea of sinful human nature seemed to be borne out in practice, while J. R. R. Tolkien's poem 'Mythopoeia', written in 1931, points out the consequences of human sin:

> I will not walk with your progressive apes,
> Erect and sapient. Before them gapes
> the dark abyss to which their progress tends.[11]

Nobody knew at this point the depths of depravity and cruelty that would be created by the rise of Nazism and Stalinism later in the 1930s. Yet Tolkien rightly saw that everything rests on the moral character of human beings, a theme he explored with particular acuity in his Lord of the Rings trilogy.

Thinking further

It was a normal service at the local church where I and my family worshipped. A student pastor, who was attached to the congregation for a few weeks to gain some experience, had been invited to give a talk to children on why selfishness is a bad thing. After saying some very predictable things in a very dull way, he invited the children to come to the front of the church, where he had a box of chocolates. He checked carefully to make sure that there were enough to go round, and then gave the box to one of the youngsters.

'I'm giving you these chocolates! Now what are you going to do with them? There are enough for each of you to have one! And if there are any left over, you could give them to the grown-ups! That would be the right thing to do, wouldn't it?'

'I suppose so . . .' the child replied. 'You're really giving them to me?' The well-meaning student nodded, smiling. He was quite unprepared for the child's reply. 'Thanks, but I'm keeping them for myself.'

The child went back to his seat and started to eat the chocolates. The crestfallen student pastor looked on in despair. The second half of his talk was to have been entitled 'The joy of generosity'. Wisely, he decided to abandon it. He hadn't scripted anything on 'The sin of selfishness'.

Christians have always recognized that sin is part of the human condition. The New Testament portrays it in several ways – such as a force that captures the human mind and will, a blindness that prevents us from seeing things as they really are, and guilt resulting from a failure to act properly. Although 'sin' is sometimes used in the sense of 'an individual action' (as we saw above), the New Testament tends to think of it primarily as a condition that leads to the commission of sin. We are slaves of sin (Romans 7.14), in the sense that we are held captive by sin, a force from which we cannot break free unaided.

It may be helpful to think of sin as an illness that has moral, relational and existential consequences. This approach builds on the healing ministry of Jesus of Nazareth, particularly his comment 'Those who are well have no need of a physician, but those who are sick; I have come to call not the righteous but sinners' (Mark 2.17). Suppose I had an illness that made me cough constantly in a way that was irritating for those around me. Not unreasonably, they might ask me to stop coughing! But I would have a problem. My coughing wouldn't be something I could really control. It would be a symptom of my illness, and although I might find a way of suppressing things, the only effective way of stopping my cough would be to cure the illness that caused it in the first place.

This analogy brings out the point that individual sins arise from a sinful disposition. Or, to put it another way, acts of sin are symptoms of the real problem, which is our sinful state. To tell someone to 'become good' is a bit like telling a lame woman to start running. She might want to do so, but she is just not capable of moving swiftly unaided. The phrase 'original sin' is sometimes used to refer to the idea of having a sinful disposition from birth, which locks us into a pattern of bad behaviour. Some would suggest that sin is guilt, while others would argue that sin is better seen as an illness that causes guilt as one of its symptoms: our sinful condition leads us to do things that are wrong, and thus incur guilt. Our sinful condition also leads us to be alienated from God, and thus fail to become the people we could be.

How are we to make sense of this? Augustine of Hippo found the analogy of a biased set of scales helpful in explaining how human beings retain freedom on the one hand while being disposed towards evil on the other. We weigh things up and decide what to do. But what, Augustine asks, if the scales are loaded towards making self-centred decisions? They will still work, but they will give us bad results.

Augustine knew only too well that human beings tend to be self-centred. Why do we abuse our God-given freedom? Because our sinful nature leads us to see things wrongly and make bad decisions. This bias towards evil – or the lesser good, as Augustine occasionally puts it – is not something that can be corrected by education. Telling us to be good won't help. We need to be *healed*, and then supported in our convalescence by the community of the Church, as we begin to adapt to the new way of life that results. The Christian gospel is what heals us – or at least what gets the process of healing started. The gospel is not a call to some form of moralism, a list of demands that we must meet; it is an invitation to be renewed and transformed, so that we want to do what is right. The gospel restores a proper way of seeing things, helping us mend the biased scales of judgement on the one hand, and renewing our will to serve God on the other.

There's another way of thinking about sin that some readers may find helpful. Sin is about separation. Yes, it's more than that – but the notion of separation really helps us to get our minds around what sin is all about. For a start, it's about separation from God (Isaiah 59.2). This theme of separation is also significant in the story of the expulsion of Adam and Eve from the garden of Eden (Genesis 3.23–24). They would not be allowed to return to paradise, or experience again the intimate presence of God. The Old Testament prophets also portrayed sin as a barrier between humanity and God, expressed physically in the architecture of the Temple in Jerusalem by the heavy woven curtain or veil that separated the people from the Holy of Holies.

Many Christian writers have picked up on the significance of the tearing or rending of this curtain at the time of the death of Christ on the cross (Matthew 27.51). This is widely interpreted as indicating that the barrier between humanity and God is removed by the death of Christ (Hebrews 10.19–22). J. C. Ryle, a nineteenth-century bishop of Liverpool who gained a reputation as a powerful preacher, had some important things to say about this:

> The rending of the veil proclaimed the termination and passing away of the ceremonial law. It was a sign that the old dispensation of sacrifices and ordinances was no longer needed. Its work was done from the moment that Christ died. There was no more need of an earthly high priest, a mercy seat, a sprinkling of blood, an offering up of incense, and a day of atonement. The true High Priest had at length appeared. The true Lamb of God had been slain. The true mercy seat was at length revealed. The figures and shadows were no longer needed.[12]

Yet the image of separation helps us think about sin in other ways. For example, Paul speaks of God reconciling the world in Christ. As we saw in *Lord and Saviour: Jesus of Nazareth*, the idea of reconciliation is about the restoration of a broken relationship. Two people become separated from each other; redemption is about restoration of the relationship, enabling the two people to come together again. Their separation is over. Sin is about separation from God; redemption is about coming back to God – just like the prodigal son returning to his waiting father. Or we can think of sin as separation from our true destiny. As we have seen in this chapter, our true destiny is to embrace and be embraced by a living and loving God. Sin is about separation from this God; redemption is about being able to achieve what we were created for in the first place.

Despite what I have just been saying, some readers may still feel that Christians make rather too much fuss about sin. After all, most worship services include some form of public confession. Surely this is unhelpful? Isn't it just getting obsessed with sin when we ought to be thinking about more positive matters? Let me try to set things in perspective. The Christian gospel – a word that means 'good news' – is not that we are sinful. The gospel is about the proclamation of hope and joy through the life, death and resurrection of Jesus of Nazareth, which we embrace through faith. It is about the life-changing realization that 'the LORD has comforted his people, and will have compassion on his suffering ones' (Isaiah 49.13). It is the confident expectation of eternal life, grounded not on our own assurance or achievements but on the gracious gift of a loving God.

Where does sin come into this? Well, when we reflect on what God has done for us, we realize what a mess we were in. The light of the gospel exposes the shadows of sin. The Christian gospel enables us to see ourselves as we really are – sinful, yet beloved of God. The same faith that embraces the promises of a loving God comes to grasp the darkness, shallowness, distortions and failings of our previous way of life. The Christian faith enables us to see that something is wrong with us, and to name the problem – sin.

Some preachers try to begin by convincing us of sin and then showing how the Christian faith is able to deal with this. There is something to be said for this approach. In some ways it is like trying to prove the existence of God so that preaching the good news about God's love is more plausible. Yet, as we noted earlier, the 'god' whose existence is proved by reason is rather anaemic in comparison with the 'God and father of our Lord Jesus Christ'. Similarly, to argue from 'sin' to the need for redemption often involves persuading people that they are immoral or failures, and then attempting to relate this to the Christian idea of sin. But this can easily lead to misunderstandings of what the Christian faith is all about. Sin is something that needs to be understood from the perspective of faith.

So how are our eyes opened so that we can perceive what the problem really is? How can we break free from a culture of denial that stops us from seeing ourselves as we really are? The New Testament makes it clear that spiritual blindness requires a spiritual cure. We need to be reborn and renewed through the work of the Holy Spirit (Titus 3.4–7) in order to see ourselves as sinners and Christ as our Saviour.

As we shall explore in the next chapter, the Christian answer to the problem of sin lies largely in the idea of grace.

3

Grace: the gift of a courteous God

When I was young, I used to love reading fairy stories. I still have some of the books that so enthralled me back in the late 1950s, as I began to develop a fondness for inhabiting imaginary worlds. One story in particular stuck in my mind. It was about a king who wished to marry his daughter to her most eligible suitor. There was no shortage of men determined to win the princess's love and the king's approval, despite having to fight dragons and giants along the way. The moral of the story was clear: love is based on achievement. Not a very romantic idea, you might think, but one that lies at the heart of Western culture. You don't get anything for nothing.

This philosophy can find its way into the life of faith. Some Christians think and act as if God's favour has to be earned. It's as if God is some mildly corrupt public official who needs to be bribed to get something done. Or a monarch surrounded by courtiers, and in order to gain access to the king you need to get the support of one of the courtiers and persuade him to plead your case. Yet no matter how natural such ways of thinking may be, they do not fit with that of the New Testament. It refers to the Christian gospel as the 'good news of God's grace' (Acts 20.24), and in this chapter we will explore what this word 'grace' might mean, and how it challenges the common-sense idea of salvation as some-thing we are asked to earn through achievement.

What is grace?

'Grace is *favour*, the free and undeserved help that God gives us to respond to his call to become children of God, adoptive sons, partakers of the divine nature and of eternal life.'[1] This helpful definition emphasizes that salvation is not something gained by merit but something bestowed by a generous and gracious God. God gives us gifts – including that of the Holy Spirit, who in turn brings spiritual gifts that deepen our faith and commitment (1 Corinthians 12.7–11).

For many of us, the idea of favour just doesn't fit with the cultural values we experience around us. If I want someone to do something for me, I'll have to do something for him. If we want to ingratiate ourselves with God, we'll have to make ourselves holy and do lots of good works. It's a natural way of thinking, deeply embedded in what scholars call 'folk-religion'. In order for God to love us, we have to make ourselves lovable first.

However, as we saw when we were thinking about the doctrine of the Trinity, God is very good at not fitting into our categories or behaving according to our expectations! A living truth, which is too great for us to see fully, cannot but sweep away our preconceptions. The doctrine of grace is one area where divine reality and human expectations collide!

One of the great themes of the Old Testament is that God loved the people of Israel not because they were great, but because God was loving. As the history of Israel makes embarrassingly clear, Israel kept getting things wrong and messing things up. Yet God still loved her, as a parent loves a child.

The story of the exodus of Israel from Egypt and Israel's eventual entry into the Promised Land is a wonderful and complex narrative of divine grace and human response. God saw that the people were suffering in Egypt. They cried out for deliverance. And what happened? God raised up Moses and led them out of Egypt. As they journeyed towards the Promised Land, Israel was given the Ten Commandments. Why? So that the people knew how to express and live out their faith in the God who had brought them out of Egypt.

But notice what did *not* happen. God did not give Israel the Ten Commandments and wait until the people had fallen into line with the demands of these laws before acting to deliver them. Deliverance was not a reward for Israel having agreed to do what God said, but a great demonstration of grace and love on God's part, to which Israel responded by pledging obedience to God.

It is natural for us to think of salvation in commercial terms. If you want something, you pay for it or do something to earn it. Yet the core meaning of grace is 'without cost'. God gives us what we could never afford to buy or hope to achieve. But that's not all. What we are given is a *transforming gift*. Suppose you are ill. The symptoms of this illness include self-centredness and an inability to do good. Then someone tells you there is a cure. It's expensive but it works, and as a favour he buys it for you. Now here's the point. Suppose you take this cure. What will happen? You will change.

God loves us as we are but does not leave us that way. God's gift to us is something that changes us into what our deepest instincts and longings tell us we are meant to be.

This is one of the great themes of the Christian faith, expressed especially well in some of the psalms, which both lament the human sinful condition and long for its transformation. 'Create in me a clean heart, O God, and put a new and right spirit within me' (Psalm 51.10).

The graciousness of God

We can think of grace in a number of ways. One of the most helpful is to look on it as a personal quality – graciousness (encompassing kindness, courtesy and compassion) – as this invites us to focus on personal relationships and the way we behave towards others. Indeed, many would argue that grace is better illustrated through stories than evaluated by theoretical analysis. A friend of mine had a casual and unplanned conversation with the evangelist Billy Graham some years ago and was deeply moved by the experience. 'He made me feel like I was the most important person at that moment. He really listened to me.' Part of being gracious is being attentive to an individual and valuing who he or she is, whatever that person's 'status' happens to be in the world.

We see this quality of graciousness in the Gospel accounts of encounters with Jesus of Nazareth. The fourth chapter of John's Gospel tells of a meeting between Jesus and a Samaritan woman. The full significance of this may be missed by modern readers though it is hinted at in the passage itself (see John 4.9, 27). Jesus sat down and talked with a Samaritan woman at a time when Samaritans were detested and excluded from Jewish society – regarded as untouchables. (That is why the parable of the good Samaritan is so powerful and challenging: someone who contemporary Jewish society regarded as an outcast fulfilled the requirements of the Old Testament law when its official Jewish representatives conspicuously failed to do so (Luke 10.30–37).) Furthermore, the crude patriarchy of the culture of the time meant that it was considered inappropriate for a man of standing to have a meeting with a woman. Widely seen as a source of temptation and sin, women were shunned by respectable males.

Yet Jesus spent time alone with this Samaritan woman, and a double prejudice – ethnic identity and gender – was thus confronted and overcome.

In this personal encounter, Jesus models the life of the coming kingdom, when those who have been reviled and excluded by the Jewish religious establishment will be welcomed in. 'There is no longer Jew or Greek, there is no longer slave or free, there is no longer male and female; for all of you are one in Christ Jesus' (Galatians 3.28). Paul sets out the theoretical basis of this in his letters, but Jesus actually demonstrates it in his dealings with individuals.

Perhaps the most striking aspect of this encounter is the after-effect of the graciousness shown to the woman. At the start, she saw Jesus as a kindly thirsty man; later on, she recognized his extraordinary ability to meet her own deeper thirst for meaning and acceptance. She began by seeing Jesus as someone who, like her, was tired; gradually, she realized that he was the one who was able to refresh and renew others. After their meeting, she rushed back to her town to tell others of this remarkable person she had met (John 4.28–29).

The passage makes a point that we too easily overlook. Graciousness is not simply uncritical acceptance of someone (who may well need to be challenged about his or her behaviour and attitudes). Christianity is about *transforming* people, not just being nice to them, and transformation can come through experiencing graciousness, as C. S. Lewis regularly demonstrates in the Chronicles of Narnia. The courteousness of Aslan, the noble lion of Narnia, causes the children to reappraise themselves and begin to see life in a new way. But perhaps the single best illustration of the transforming power of graciousness is the Gospel encounter between Jesus and Zacchaeus (Luke 19.1–9).

Luke's narrative makes clear that Zacchaeus is not well liked. A rich tax collector who has made his money by collaborating with the Roman imperial authorities, he has probably been inflating his demands for payment to accumulate even more on the side. Yet he is drawn to Jesus of Nazareth. We are not told why. Is it that he is longing for liberation from his entrapment to wealth? That he has not found his heart's desire and senses that Jesus might be the answer? We simply don't know. The narrative tells us nothing about his motives. Its focus is on the graciousness of Jesus and the impact this has on Zacchaeus. 'Zacchaeus, hurry and come down; for I must stay at your house today.'

Those hearing Jesus' affirming words are shocked. Doesn't he know that Zacchaeus is a tax collector? A notorious sinner? Someone to be avoided? Surely showing such graciousness condones collaboration and extortion! Yet it proves to be transformative. 'Look, half of my possessions, Lord, I will give to the poor; and if I have defrauded anyone of anything, I will pay back four times as much.'

A major theological principle is conveyed in this moving story. *Salvation is grace, and ethics is gratitude.* Having found acceptance with Jesus, Zacchaeus responds by expressing his new status through changed attitudes and actions. We ought to be challenged by this. Surely Zacchaeus should have repented before Jesus accepted him? Yet the narrative is quite clear: transformation is the consequence, not the precondition or cause, of acceptance in the sight of Jesus. Grace comes first, and is followed by obedience.

Adoption: gracious acceptance into a community

In *Lord and Saviour: Jesus of Nazareth*, we looked at a range of New Testament images of salvation. One image that we did not have space to discuss in that volume is of particular relevance to thinking about God's grace. The image of adoption is used by Paul to express the distinction between believers as 'sons of God' and Jesus of Nazareth as 'the Son of God' (Romans 8.15, 8.23, 9.4; Galatians 4.5). The image is drawn from the sphere of Roman family law, with which Paul (and many of his readers) would have been familiar.[2]

Under this law, the head of a family (*paterfamilias*) was free to adopt individuals – almost invariably males – from outside his natural family, and give them the legal status of adoption. This had three consequences for the adopted person. First, it meant that all his existing debts would be cancelled; second, he would be granted the same inheritance rights as the natural children; and third, he would take on the name of the adopting family and have the same social status as its other members. In ancient Rome, this third point was of no small importance, given the influence of leading Roman families.

It's easy to see why Paul found this Roman legal procedure to be such a good analogy for the altered standing of believers. Through faith, believers come to have the same status as Jesus of Nazareth (although this does not imply we have the same divine nature – we can be 'sons of God' without being the 'son of God'). We are adopted into the family of God, with all the benefits that this brings. Most importantly, Paul sees adoption as an act of grace, something that is wrought by the Holy Spirit working within us. Adoption is about the conferring of privileges – privileges that we do not deserve yet God graciously bestows upon us.

First, adoption involves the cancellation of debts. In the Roman context, an adopted son would often come from a poorer family, and might even have been sold into some form of slavery – typically as a 'bondsman', whereby he would have agreed to serve a household for a period of several years for a certain sum. The process of adoption involved the *paterfamilias* settling all debts, effectively liberating the son from his obligations by buying his freedom.

It's easy to see the important point that Paul is making. In adopting us, God cancels our debts. Everything in our past that prevents us becoming 'sons of God' is dealt with. Debts are cancelled. Our freedom is secured. We are given a new status at two levels. First, because our past is set behind us. And second, because we share in the reputation and prestige of a noble family. That's why Paul speaks about the 'freedom of the glory of the children of God' (Romans 8.21).

Second, adoption involves receiving inheritance rights. To be a member of the household of faith is to be an heir of God. Believers are thus 'heirs of God' and 'joint heirs with Christ' (Romans 8.17), in that we share in the same inheritance rights as Jesus. He suffered and was glorified, and this may be our expectation, too. All that Jesus has inherited from God will one day be ours as well. For Paul, this insight helps us cope with suffering. Jesus suffered before he was glorified; believers must expect to do the same.

Third, adoption into the family of God brings a new sense of belonging. We are now part of a new household and family, and we take on a new name that reflects our new identity. We all need to feel that we belong somewhere: social psychologists have demonstrated the necessity of a 'secure base', a community or group that gives people a sense of purpose and an awareness of being valued and loved by others. In human terms, we have the family unit; in Christian terms, we are adopted into the family of God. We can rest assured that we are valued within this family, and this gives us the self-confidence to work in and witness to the world.

This third aspect of adoption has become increasingly helpful in our generation, as fragmentation within Western culture leads many people to feel they do not belong anywhere. There is a pervasive sense of being lost, displaced, adrift, and a yearning to have somewhere to call home. To be adopted into the family of faith is to be welcomed into a grand household and to enjoy the change of status that adoption brings: we matter; we are wanted; we are valuable.

This insight lies behind a story told by Ambrose (339–97), a bishop of Milan during the time that Christianity was the official state religion of the Roman Empire. Ambrose's story goes back to the Valerian persecution of 258, which decreed that all Christians who had been formally denounced were to be executed and their goods confiscated by the imperial treasury. After martyring Sixtus II, the pope of the time, the prefect of Rome tried to find where the churches had concealed their riches. He summoned Laurence, one of the deacons of Rome, and instructed him to return with the spoils within three days. In fact, Laurence came back with a small group of church members. These, he declared, were the true treasure of the Church. The prefect was not amused, and Laurence was executed shortly afterwards. Ambrose's account of this incident makes a powerful theological point about the new status of believers, granted by grace.

> For when the treasure of the Church was demanded from [Laurence], he promised that he would present them. On the following day he brought together the poor. When he was asked where the promised treasure was, he pointed to the poor, saying: 'These are the treasure of the Church.' And they really were treasures – those in whom Christ lives, in whom there is faith in Him. As the Apostle says: 'we have this treasure in clay jars' (2 Corinthians 4.7). What greater treasure has Christ than those in whom he declares that he lives?[3]

Being reassured that God really is gracious

One of my favourite theologians of the twentieth century – now widely regarded as one of the greatest of his age – was Thomas F. Torrance (1913–2007). Torrance was born in China to Scottish missionary parents, and returned to Edinburgh to study theology. Near the end of his life, I wrote his biography[4] and as a result spent a lot of time with him, hearing memories of his ministry and discussing the development of his ideas. One period of Torrance's life was clearly of great importance to him: the several years he spent as a chaplain to a Scottish regiment during the Second World War, initially in the Middle East and then in Italy. A memory that stood out was a question raised by a young soldier whom he found lying on the ground, mortally wounded in battle. As Torrance offered what help he could, the soldier asked him whether God was 'really like Jesus'. Torrance assured him that this was so. The young man died a few moments later.

Torrance told me that this episode had brought home to him how important it is to be able to reassure people that God may be fully known through Jesus of Nazareth. In *The Christian Doctrine of God*, he put it like this:

> There is only the one God who has revealed himself in Jesus Christ in such a way that there is perfect consistency and fidelity between what he reveals of the Father and what the Father is in his unchangeable reality.[5]

We need not fear that God is 'one thing in himself and another thing in Jesus Christ', for in Jesus, 'the whole fullness of deity dwells bodily' (Colossians 2.9). There is no 'dark inscrutable God' hidden behind the gracious and loving face of Jesus of Nazareth.

Torrance took great comfort from this insight and talked about it at several of our meetings. However, it wasn't until something happened to me a few years later that I really appreciated its importance. I had been attending a series of meetings in London to set up some lectures. There were only a few of us involved, including someone who was invariably polite and helpful, and after our second meeting I mentioned to a colleague how impressed I was with this person. My colleague looked me straight in the eye. 'I don't think you really know him. There's something not quite right there.' My colleague was correct. At the third meeting, someone said something that enraged this person. He began to scream and shout, and after telling us exactly what he thought of us he ran out of the room, slamming the door behind him. There was an embarrassed silence before we just got back to the business of arranging the lectures.

What this incident revealed was that there was a public face to this man and a private reality, which nobody was meant to see. And once we had glimpsed the darker side of his nature, we could never forget it. This was what he was really like. Up to that point we had been presented with a façade, shielding us from the unpleasantness that lay beneath. Many readers will have little difficulty recalling similar encounters.

God isn't like this rather Jekyll and Hyde character, pretending to be nice and hoping we don't discover the truth. No. The God we encounter in Jesus of Nazareth is both the true God and the truth about God. That's why Torrance's insight is so important. The gracious and loving God whom we see in the face of Jesus is not a consoling delusion that we have invented or a deception that is being imposed on us. Jesus shows us the fullness of God so that God's character and nature can be definitively seen and known. He brings the Old Testament to fulfilment, not just in the sense of being the one to whom it points, but also in enabling us to understand it properly.

In the words of Augustine of Hippo, Jesus of Nazareth removes the veil that partially conceals the true meaning of the Old Testament. Paul – in speaking of those who continue to read the Old Testament law as a demand for obedience rather than a promise of redemption – writes, 'A veil lies over their minds; but when one turns to the Lord, the veil is removed' (2 Corinthians 3.15–16). It is possible to read the Old Testament as a narrative of a tribal God who demands total obedience to a legalistic code. But as Paul and Augustine both realized, this is a false reading of the text. When read rightly, in the light of Christ, the Old Testament is revealed as a narrative of God's promises of redemption, which are fulfilled in Jesus of Nazareth. So, although some may persist in regarding the Old Testament as a collection of totally unreasonable legal demands, Christians rightly see it as a promise of grace.

Martin Luther is one of many believers who discovered a gracious God after previously thinking of God as a taskmaster who set impossible tasks for people to fulfil. I began my career as a theologian by studying Luther's theological development, and found it fascinating to track and understand his changing ideas.[6] Towards the end of his life, Luther wrote about a spiritual crisis he went through in his 20s, sparked off by Paul's declaration that the righteousness of God is revealed in the gospel (Romans 1.17).

Why would this verse cause a crisis? Because of the way that Luther interpreted it, as a demand for righteousness on the part of sinners as a precondition for being accepted by God. No righteousness, no salvation. Luther had a very low opinion of his own holiness and couldn't see what hope was there for someone like him – trapped in sin, unable either to break free from its grip or to become a virtuous person. He became convinced that salvation was impossible – for himself, at least.

Then he began to realize that he had misunderstood what Paul meant. When Paul talked about God's righteousness being revealed in the gospel, he was not speaking about a legalistic demand that God imposes on us but rather the righteousness that God graciously gives us, in order that we can be righteous before God. Luther's understanding underwent a big change. No wonder he spoke of this passage as a wonderful new way of grasping what righteousness is!

A debate about grace: the Pelagian controversy

In *Lord and Saviour: Jesus of Nazareth*, we noted how Christian reflection on the best way of understanding the identity and significance of Jesus of Nazareth was sparked by the Arian controversy of the fourth century. A similar thing happened with Christian thinking about grace. In this case, a debate took place in the early fifth century between Augustine of Hippo, based in Roman North Africa, and Pelagius, a British ascetic who had settled in Rome. Pelagius was concerned about the lax morals he found within Roman Christianity, and attributed these partly to the ideas of Augustine.

Augustine was converted to Christianity in August 386. He was convinced that this was not a matter of his own choosing, and as he reflected on the apparent coincidences that led him to faith he became convinced that he discerned the grace of God preceding him at every point, nudging him towards the critical moment of conversion. Augustine frequently expresses his profound sense of being totally dependent on God. 'My whole hope is only in your mercy. Give what you command, and command what you will.' For Augustine, a sinful and fractured humanity desperately needed a gracious and loving God, just as a wounded and damaged patient needs the ministrations of a caring and competent physician.

Pelagius read Augustine's *Confessions* in Rome in about 405. He was appalled when he came to: 'Give what you command, and command what you will.' These words seemed to strike at the heart of Pelagius' attempts to reform Roman Christianity, suggesting that human beings were under no obligation to seek perfection.

Pelagius asserted that we are completely free in all our actions. We are not influenced by hidden forces, nor are we restricted by powers that lie beyond our control. We are the masters of our own destiny, and if we are told to stop sinning we can stop sinning: sin is something that we can and must resist. God has given us the Ten Commandments and the example of Jesus Christ, and it's up to us to live according to them. As Pelagius saw it, any imperfection in human nature that might stop us acting morally would reflect badly on God. As God made us, it would be insulting to God, as well as to us, to suggest that we have some inbuilt fault. It would suggest that God didn't create us particularly well.

Augustine, however, argued that the New Testament, especially the writings of Paul, seemed to be saying something rather different. For Augustine, Pelagius' views on human nature were dangerously naïve and bore little relation to either the New Testament teaching or human experience. Augustine's basic belief is that human nature, although created without any problems, is contaminated by sin as a result of the fall. In other words, we have a flaw that wasn't there when God created us – an inherent bias towards acts of sinning that contaminates our lives from birth and dominates them thereafter.

Augustine develops an idea already found in Paul's letters. The law is able to tell us what we ought to do, although it doesn't actually help us do what is good. It can help us to *name* sin, although not actually to avoid it (Romans 7.7–20), in the way that knowing what a problem is doesn't actually help us solve it. There is something about human nature that inclines it to do things it knows to be wrong. We need help from outside our own situation.

Augustine argues that we are trapped by sin and unable to break free from its power. Some mysterious fascinating force is attracting us like a magnet and we can only struggle ineffectually against it. If left on our own, we will just become more deeply embedded in our situation, like a truck stuck in mud. The more we spin our wheels, the further down we'll go. We need someone to pull us out.

Or it might be helpful to think of our enthralment to sin as being in prison. The mere knowledge that you're in jail isn't enough to set you free, though. Someone has to get you out. She might blast the jail open, or she might just turn a key in the door lock – but either way, someone else needs to intervene if you are to gain your liberty.

Pelagius argues that we are not trapped in any situation. We are the masters of our own destiny. If we are told to stop sinning, we can stop sinning. Sin is something that we can and must resist. We can take charge of our lives, and achieve whatever goals we set ourselves. Pelagius, like the subject of William Ernest Henley's poem 'Invictus', a great favourite with the Victorians, believed:

> I am the master of my fate:
> I am the captain of my soul.

Pelagius gained many supporters at Rome who saw his reforms as sanctified common sense. What exactly was the problem with demanding moral improvement from people? Pelagius was offering a sophisticated vision of self-improvement with a strong spiritual core, based on the teaching and moral example of Jesus of Nazareth. For these people, Christianity was really a religion of self-help and self-improvement, with Jesus as an inspiring example rather than a transforming Saviour.

Augustine, on the other hand, held that the only way we are ever going to get free is by being realistic about our situation. Sin traps humanity within nature, allowing us freedom within this sphere of activity but preventing us from breaking free from it to encounter the living God. Through grace, God opens our eyes and ears and liberates us from the limitations of our natural condition so we can recognize and respond to his gracious call.

Augustine's understanding of Christianity is dominated by the thought of the grace of God. Perhaps his favourite text is 'Apart from me, you can do nothing' (John 15.5). Christ's death and resurrection break the power of sin and cancel its guilt. Christ is the second Adam, the one who came to restore us to fellowship with God and empower us to keep the law. As Augustine himself puts it,

> Grace is not just knowledge of the divine law or our own nature or the forgiveness of sins. It is something which is given to us through our Lord Jesus Christ so that by it the law may be fulfilled, nature delivered and sin defeated.

The debate between Augustine and Pelagius is often revisited by Christians. On the one hand, Pelagius' emphasis on the importance of trying to do our best is welcomed. On the other, Augustine's emphasis on human frailty fits in far better with the New Testament's stress on God's graciousness towards us. For Augustine, human beings are damaged, wounded and seriously ill. There is no point in demanding that we improve ourselves when the essence of our condition is that we are trapped in our predicament. Pelagius seems to be in denial about the human situation. His naïve approach, although unquestionably well intentioned, could be compared to ordering a blind man to see things properly. Spiritual healing, not simply moral direction, is required.

We can appreciate that Augustine sees a frail and vulnerable humanity as dependent on a gracious God for its wellbeing and salvation. But is this a healthy outlook? In the final section of this chapter, we shall consider some concerns that have been raised about this view.

Grace and dependency: an unhealthy relationship?

The movement we call the Enlightenment (or Age of Reason) was critical of Augustine's approach to human nature. Many of its writers argued that he was devaluing human abilities and quoted a famous aphorism of the pre-Socratic philosopher Protagoras: 'Humanity is the measure of all things.'[7] The Age of Reason presupposed the reliability of human moral judgement and standards of rationality.

Possibly things were rather simpler back in the eighteenth century. Nowadays, looking at the havoc caused by world wars and the immense suffering brought about by the inhumane ways in which we have treated one another, it seems much easier to believe that there is something wrong with us. The German philosopher Nietzsche argued that life is not governed by rational principles; rather, we have to accept that it is full of cruelty, injustice, uncertainty and absurdity. There are no absolute standards of good and evil that can be demonstrated by human reason.

Others, however, would argue that the real problem with Augustine's approach is that it encourages an attitude of servile dependence on God. Nietzsche championed this criticism of faith. 'Christianity has taken the side of everything weak and lowly,' he declared. 'It has made an ideal out of opposition to the instinct of strong life.'[8] Instead of standing up for themselves and valuing strength and power, Christians celebrate weakness and dependence.

Now there is something in what Nietzsche is saying here. Some Christians probably do get locked into unhelpful patterns of dependency. But it doesn't have to be this way. What the Christian idea of grace affirms is that God does not leave us alone to confront the challenges of life, but acts to free us from the power of sin and guilt throughout our Christian lives. At one point, Paul relates how he found himself in a situation of utter helplessness, in which he became acutely aware of his own weakness. He recalls how he took comfort from the Lord's words, 'My grace is sufficient for you, for power is made perfect in weakness' (2 Corinthians 12.9).

This Christian sense of dependence on a gracious God is best expressed in prayer. Pelagianism never really came to terms with the way in which prayer clearly points to a loving dependence on God, such as a child might show in holding on to its mother in a moment of need, distress, or danger. As Augustine realized, prayer means that we are not totally dependent on our own resources. Yes, we do our best – but then we let God do the rest. Prayer expresses a fundamental aspect of the Christian understanding of grace: when we have exhausted our own resources, we can draw on a strength that lies beyond us. As Augustine put it,

> Christ is your salvation, so fix your mind on Christ. Accept his cup of salvation, for he heals all your diseases . . . Your life has been redeemed from corruption; there is no need to be afraid any more.[9]

Is this deluded nonsense? Surely not. It is simply a recognition of the limits of humanity and the grace of God. If you're ill, you need a doctor. If your leg is broken, you need help in walking. Recognizing our frailty and sin does not in any way detract from our pursuit of virtue, or our attempt to follow the example of Jesus of Nazareth. Rather, it sets a proper context for both, reminding us that we cannot hope to achieve such goals in our own strength but need to rely on the strength and grace of God. We do our best and let God do the rest.

Augustine took the view that humanity was wounded and messed up, prone to make mistakes and get things wrong. That's why he liked to compare the Church to a hospital – a community of people who are ill but under the care of a physician. We are recovering from trauma, wounds and abuse. Together, we can help one another regain confidence, as we are healed and renewed.

Augustine's image of the Church as a hospital is worth thinking more about. In part, Augustine developed this idea through his reflections on the parable of the good Samaritan (Luke 10.25–37). Augustine saw this parable as a powerful exploration of the human dilemma and the role of the Church in healing and renewing wounded human nature. For Augustine, the wounded man left on the road is a symbol of human nature. We are wounded, abandoned and unable to help ourselves. We need someone to help us and heal us. The good Samaritan himself is an image of Jesus, who comes to our assistance in an act of graciousness and kindness. He bandages our wounds, pouring on healing oil and wine.

Yet we need to remember that the parable does not end with the Samaritan coming to the aid of the wounded man. He entrusts the man to an innkeeper and leaves him under his care until he will return. For Augustine, the redemption that is achieved by Christ is accompanied by being entrusted to the care of a community. The community of faith was to be seen as an extension and continuation of the saving and healing work of Christ our Redeemer.

This naturally leads us to think more about the community of faith. What do the creeds have to say about the place of the Church in the Christian life?

4

The Church: the communion of saints

All of us have memories of meetings that have left a deep impression on us. I remember visiting an old lady while I was a curate in Nottingham in the early 1980s. She was unwell and thought she had not much longer to live. 'I'm looking forward to going home,' she told me. I was new in my job and didn't quite catch the significance of what she was saying. Happily, she realized this and explained what she meant. 'I look forward to being in heaven. That's the hope that keeps me going.' It was a powerful statement, and I wove it into my sermon at her funeral a year later.

But that was only part of what the elderly lady said to me that cold and wet afternoon, as we drank strong tea together in her snug kitchen. She lived on her own; her husband had died ten years earlier. 'The church is my family,' she told me. It was where she felt she belonged. Then she used another phrase that stuck in my mind. 'It's like an outpost of heaven.' Her church seemed to her to be a foretaste, no matter how inadequate, of what heaven would be like. She felt it was a threshold from which she could dimly see what lay beyond.

Many of us think about the Church as a community, which offers us support and encouragement and helps us follow

Christ. This old lady realized it was also a pointer, a signpost, to something greater. In the next two chapters, we shall look at this theme and some others and see how they fit into the life of faith. But let's stay for now with the clear insight we find in the New Testament, played out over two thousand years of Christian history: ours is not a solitary faith but one lived out in the company of others.

The community of faith

The Spirit of grace inhabits a community, not simply a collection of individuals. By the one Spirit, Christians throughout the world are all baptized into the body of Christ – the Church (1 Corinthians 12.13), through which the life-giving and life-changing Spirit of God can flow. But why does community matter?

Let's begin with a very simple point. I learned to play chess when I was about 6. At the start, I wasn't much good at it. I had no idea about making strategic moves and tended to rely on my opponents having even less experience of the game than I did. At 13 I moved to a new school, which had a well-established chess club. I suppose it was inevitable that I would join it. For the next four years I was an active member, and over time I noticed two things happening.

First of all, I got much better at playing chess. It wasn't just practice; it was because I could talk to older students who took chess seriously and had devoured books by grand masters. As they spoke about their strategies, I found myself beginning to grasp the game at a deeper level than before. Previously, I had just moved pieces around according to the rules; now, I played tactically, in a classic demonstration of the young learning from the older and wiser.

But I wouldn't have improved if I had not joined the chess club.

The second thing that happened grew out of this. My school had a very strong sporting tradition and an outstanding reputation in rugby, cricket and rowing. Chess was seen by most of my peers as an intellectual game, played by socially backward students who were incapable of doing anything more interesting or worthwhile. So we chess enthusiasts huddled together for comfort. Within the club there was a sense of shared values and friendship, which helped us cope with the gently critical attitude of others. It's much easier to handle marginalization in company than on your own.

I gave up playing chess when I went to university at Oxford, partly because my academic work was so interesting that it displaced the game. But after I discovered Christianity, I found the same pattern repeating itself. Going to church in Oxford helped me in two ways. First, it introduced me to people who knew a lot more about their faith that I did. Personal friendships opened the way to a deeper understanding of what the Christian faith was all about and how best to live it out. Every now and then, a sermon might prove especially exciting and help me to grasp something that had hitherto eluded me. The church was a community that stimulated my growth in faith.

But there was more to it than that. In the 1970s, Oxford students were fascinated by Marxism and tended to see any kind of religious belief or involvement as outmoded and reactionary. Why read about Jesus of Nazareth when you could read Mao Tse-tung's Little Red Book? Churches were essential to resisting such transient cultural trends. They acted as communities of support and encouragement in the face of hostility, indifference and cynicism. They provided fellowship, mutual support and encouragement. They were like spiritual oases in the midst of a wilderness or desert, offering refreshment and revitalization. Of course, we all know that churches can go wrong and become inward-looking, suspicious and oppressive. But when they work, they're great.

How can we understand more of what the Church is all about? One of the best ways is to look at a series of analogies or images for the Church that we find in the New Testament, and to explore the tradition of Christian reflection on this text. Let's begin with the idea of the Church as a people who have been called together by God.

Being called out of the world

I often find myself being struck by certain biblical verses, lingering over them and taking delight in their ideas and images. One that regularly slows me down is a short statement in John's Gospel, in which Jesus speaks of his coming death. 'I, when I am lifted up from the earth, will draw all people to myself' (John 12.32). There is much to reflect on here, including the subtle reworking of a theme associated with the 'Suffering Servant': 'he shall be exalted and lifted up, and shall be very high' (Isaiah 52.13). Where some might take this 'exaltation' to refer to preferment or promotion, here it is reinterpreted as being raised up on the cross. That's interesting, but it's not the main thing that causes me to slow down.

The fact is there's a deep understanding of the Church packed into that verse: it presents the Church as the community that gathers around the crucified Christ. We can see the beginnings of this community in those who assembled around the cross at Calvary, and its extension in Paul's equation of the gospel with the 'message of the cross'. The compelling image of Jesus of Nazareth suffering on the cross invokes in us something that cannot really be put into words. The Church is those who gather together around Christ, believing that they have been called to follow him.

The Greek word *ekklēsia*, traditionally translated as 'church', refers to an assembly of people, convened for a purpose. During the Golden Age of ancient Athens, an assembly of citizens was convened in times of need – for example, at moments of political crisis, when a decision had to be made about whether to go to war, or to elect representatives.

The New Testament sees the Church as such an assembly of Christians, called by God 'out of darkness into his marvellous light' (1 Peter 2.9). It is not an accidental construct that Christians blunder into, but a centre of support, encouragement and teaching; it is not primarily a human invention, but a community that is saturated by grace and inhabited by the Holy Spirit. All Christian writers – whether Protestant, Catholic or Orthodox – consider the Church to be an integral part of the Christian life. Initially, Christians seem to have used the word 'church' to refer simply to a gathering of believers, likely to meet in a private house for prayer and worship. When the New Testament speaks of the church at Corinth or Philippi, it means a 'house church', a relatively small group of people.

Once Christianity became a legal religion (with the conversion of Constantine in 313), a subtle change began to take place. As they were no longer forced to meet in secret, Christians could begin to construct their own buildings for public worship. Gradually, the word 'church' came to refer to the buildings in which Christians assembled, not the assembly of believers itself. In our own day, it is used to refer to a Christian organization – for example, the Church of England or the Methodist Church. This emphasis on the institutional or organizational aspects of Christianity, rather than the ideas and values that lie at the heart of the Christian faith, is quite natural. Christians need to meet somewhere, and they need to organize themselves if they are to survive.

Let's continue our thinking about the nature of the Church by exploring the strengths and weaknesses of some traditional models.[1] Some of these have associations with particular Christian denominations, while others emphasize certain aspects of the role of the Church. Taken together, they can help us begin to put into words some of the core ideas that underlie our Christian understanding.

The Church: a secure base for the Christian life

A few years ago, I researched and wrote a biography of C. S. Lewis. One of the things I discovered was how unhappy Lewis was at school. Following his mother's death in 1908, shortly before Lewis's tenth birthday, his father sent him away from home to study at English boarding schools. Although it was probably a well-meant decision, it turned out to be disastrous for Lewis's personal development. He was separated from most of his family and closest friends.

Others knew the same experience. In 1951, the British psychologist John Bowlby (1907–90) produced a study for the World Health Organization that looked at the mental health problems of children who had been displaced by the Second World War. His main conclusion was that children needed a 'secure base' from which they could learn to cope with challenges, develop independence and mature emotionally.[2]

This idea of a 'secure base' is helpful as we think about the creeds. One of the great themes of the Old Testament is that God is a place of safety and refuge. Christians can find refuge in the shadow of God's wings (Psalm 36.7). God is like a strong tower, a fortress or a place of safety. It's an idea that is familiar to many through Augustus M. Toplady's famous hymn 'Rock of Ages, cleft for me'. God is portrayed as a secure base, a rock on which we may stand, even when the storms of life rage around us.

Yet this idea is also helpful in thinking about the nature of the Church. The Church is a community that enfolds us, protects us and encourages us as we grow in our faith. It is like a nursery that helps us set down roots and grow. One day, we can look after ourselves. Yet we need a place in which we can explore our faith and test its limits, make mistakes, and learn from them. It's no accident that many Christians find it helpful to talk about the Church as a 'mother'. It's an image that can be traced back to Cyprian of Carthage in the third century. 'You can't have God as your father,' he remarked, 'unless you have the Church as your mother.'[3] John Calvin made much the same point in the sixteenth century:

> I shall start, then, with the church, into whose bosom God is pleased to gather his sons, not only that they may be nourished by her help and ministry as long as they are infants and children, but also that they may be guided by her motherly care until they mature and at last reach the goal of faith.[4]

Now we all know that churches can go wrong. It's a sad fact of life that churches can be places of bullying and abuse.

But they're not meant to be like this, and they don't have to be like this. They can be places of security, hospitality and care.

Traditional models of the Church

One of the most familiar ways of thinking about the Church is to see it as an institution, and for many in the secular world this has become the default option. When Constantine was converted and believers were given the opportunity to meet openly for the first time, the strength of Christianity on the ground became increasingly obvious. Christianity began to play a greater role in imperial politics, eventually becoming the official religion of the Roman Empire. When, in the fifth century, the Roman Empire began to collapse in Western Europe, the Christian Church emerged as the only institution to survive the chaos that followed the breakdown of imperial rule. There are obviously limits to the comparison, but the Western Church began to see itself as the successor to the Roman Empire, with the pope as the new emperor and the bishops as the new governors of provinces.

The benefits of this model were obvious. By the Middle Ages, the Church was the most stable and influential institution in Western Europe. But it had its weaknesses. Some felt that it had lost touch with its historical and spiritual roots in the New Testament and had become preoccupied with issues of power and money. Many such issues were debated in the sixteenth century, which was an age of Reformation for the churches in Western Europe.

But perhaps not addressed as thoroughly as they might have been were (a) the danger of attaching too much importance to preserving the institution of the Church at the expense of other legitimate concerns, and (b) the way in which renewal movements can be suppressed and charismatic voices marginalized if they appear to challenge traditional, institutional ways of thinking.

Another way of regarding the Church is to see it as a community of faith. This idea is often expressed in terms of Paul's powerful image of the 'body of Christ' (see especially 1 Corinthians 12), which suggests an interconnected body of people, each of whom has a role to play in sustaining the ministry of the Church. To speak of the Church as the 'God's people' (1 Peter 2.10) is not to deny the importance of individuals or human individuality; it is to recognize that individuals are enabled to grow in wisdom and to overcome their limitations through belonging to a community. As the theologian Dietrich Bonhoeffer (1906–45) realized, other people are good for us – no matter how irksome and difficult we may at times find them. They help us identify and face up to our pride, weaknesses and vanities. And as others accept us, so we come to accept others.

> A Christian fellowship lives and exists by the intercession of its members for one another, or it collapses. I can no longer condemn or hate a brother for whom I pray, no matter how much trouble he causes me. His face, that hitherto may have been strange and intolerable to me, is transformed in intercession into the countenance of a brother for whom Christ died, the face of a forgiven sinner.[5]

I was speaking at a conference of ministers in Chicago. Having an hour spare, I slipped into a session dealing with clergy burnout. Several clergy were speaking about the causes of burnout and the impact it had on their lives. More importantly, they also talked about what they found helpful in dealing with it. One of the clergy found that the biggest cause of stress was his bad relationships with other people – including other ministers and members of his own congregation. He shared what he found helpful in dealing with this problem.

He told us how he thought about people he disliked or found difficult. These are people for whom Christ died! Therefore he had to force himself to see them in that light. Instead of seeing them as people who annoyed him and made his life difficult, he would try to see them from God's perspective. God loved them – and so must he. Yet he then found something utterly transformative taking place – something unexpected, which he put down to the grace of God. He began to see people in a new way, actively seeking out their good points. And when he started looking for their good points, he found them.

Now I don't know whether that pastor had read Bonhoeffer. But he had certainly read his New Testament, especially Paul's plea that we should try to see others as being better than ourselves (Philippians 2.3). The Church is meant to be a community in which we delight in one another's strengths and help one another cope with our weaknesses. It's a community which helps us to grow in faith by providing us with support as we try, by God's grace, to become better people.

There's another point we need to make here. Faith is a great social leveller, precisely because the Christian gospel makes it clear that social status is not of any great importance in God's sight. Paul's image of the 'body of Christ' may be seen as a subtle and understated criticism of the hierarchical model of society that was prevalent throughout the Roman

Empire, in which someone's social status was largely the result of that person's circumstances. Accidents of birth were not to be carried over into the Church! The one who some in society would consider an 'inferior member' is to be given 'greater honour' within the Church (1 Corinthians 12.24). A similar point is made in the letter of James, which criticizes church leaders who prioritize rich church members over poor ones (James 2.1–4).

Yet another way of understanding the Church is to consider it as a *school of discipleship*. The later letters of the New Testament emphasize the importance of teaching, both for the transmission of faith to later generations and as a means of helping present-day Christians to develop maturity in their faith. In the early church, the bishop was often seen as having a significant role. Cyril of Jerusalem (*c.* 315–87) is widely regarded as one of the finest teachers of this period: his 'catechetical lectures' were delivered at Jerusalem in about the year 350 to those preparing for baptism. The early church took this sacrament very seriously and used the period of Lent to teach people who wished to publicly acknowledge their faith through baptism. The ceremony itself took place on Easter Day in order to celebrate the new life it brought.

Instruction is an important aspect of the Church's identity and mission. As we have stressed throughout this series of books, Christianity is not an uninformed trust in God or a blind faith in certain doctrines. It is a coherent set of ideas linked together to enable believers to make sense of life and live it to the full. As the recent rise of the New Atheism has made clear, Christians need to know what they believe and why they believe it. Although many of today's most influential Christian teachers have leadership roles in churches, some do not – perhaps the most famous of these being C. S. Lewis, who took great pleasure in emphasizing that he was simply a 'layman of the Church of England'.

This teaching role of the Church does not simply concern what Christians believe; it's about inculcating values and exploring how these can be put into practice in life. At its best, the Church is a community of wisdom, in which guidance can be given about how best to live out the Christian faith in an increasingly complex world where many of the old certainties don't seem to work well any more.

A final way of thinking about the Church is to see it as a herald – a community that tries to explain and commend its ideas and values to those outside its confines. The early church grew out of the apostolic proclamation of the gospel and saw this act as a core aspect of its identity. Those within the Church were to be helped to grow in their faith; those outside were to be enabled to understand what Christianity was all about and the difference it could make to their lives.

The use of the term 'herald' is important. A herald announces the coming of a person. The Church is the community that gathers in worship and prayer around the risen Jesus of Nazareth. Although Christianity does have certain beliefs, it is more fundamentally about a relationship with Christ. The great Baptist preacher C. H. Spurgeon (1834–92) made this point well.

> The theme of a minister should be Christ Jesus in opposition to *mere doctrine*. Some of my good brethren are always preaching doctrine. Well, they are right in so doing, but I would not care myself to have as the characteristic of my preaching, doctrine only. I would rather have it said, 'He dwelt much upon the person of Christ.'[6]

Let's explore this point further.

The Church and the world: images and insights

What is the Church? Ignatius of Antioch, who was martyred for his faith in Rome in about the year 108, had a neat answer: 'Wherever Christ is, there is the Church.' It's a nice piece of theology, and it makes a lot of sense of the New Testament's statements about the Church as the community that gathers around Jesus of Nazareth. Just as the teaching of Jesus drew crowds in Palestine, so the Church's proclamation of Jesus of Nazareth draws followers down the ages. 'Where two or three are gathered in my name, I am there among them' (Matthew 18.20). In his 1948 address to the World Council of Churches, the great Swiss theologian Karl Barth declared that the Church consists of 'the gathering together of those men and women whom the living Lord Jesus Christ chooses and calls to be witnesses of the victory he has already won, and heralds of its future manifestation'.

Although Ignatius was a bishop, with a strong sense of the value of church structures and discipline, he was clear what was of decisive importance. The centre of the life, thought and worship of the Church was Jesus of Nazareth. The institution of the Church was secondary to the person of Jesus Christ, who was its true foundation and focus. The preaching, sacraments and ministry of the Church were intended to sustain and nourish the presence of Christ within the community of faith, so that he in turn might sustain and nourish believers.

This rich idea opens up lots of interesting questions. How are we to think about believers being sustained in this way by Jesus of Nazareth? How can we think of them as growing? It is interesting to note how many Christian writers have picked up on the biblical imagery that suggests that the Church is like a vineyard, which is to be tended so that it may bear fruit. Caring for a vineyard is an excellent image for ministry (Matthew 20.1–16). In Palestine, a vineyard needed to be shielded from wild animals and the elements. It was all too easy for a vineyard to die and revert to barren soil. It needed protection and irrigation.

This led some theologians to compare the Church to a walled garden, similar to the Garden of Eden. Isaac Watts (1674–1748), best known for 'When I survey the wondrous cross', penned a hymn that expressed this idea, based on some themes from the Song of Songs:

> We are a garden walled around,
> Chosen and made peculiar ground;
> A little spot enclosed by grace
> Out of the world's wide wilderness.

It is helpful to think of the Church as an oasis within a desert, where plants can flourish, grow and bear fruit. This suggestive image weaves together the core themes of community, grace and the Holy Spirit.

Another image of the Church makes a similar point. Just as Noah's ark bore people (and animals!) through the floods to safety, so the Church, like a boat voyaging on the high seas – the sea, you will recall, is often regarded as an image of chaos and destruction in the Old Testament – represents a place of security in the face of chaos and a mode of transport to a safe haven. This idea is reflected in the architecture of many churches. The 'nave', the central part of the church, in which the congregation sits, takes its name from the Latin word for ship, *navis*, and the vaulted roof of the nave looks rather like an inverted ship's keel.

The Christian Church will always exist in tension with what we sometimes call 'the world'. As I touched on earlier, many theologians believe that Christianity lost something of its original vitality when it became entangled with power politics as part of the Roman cultural establishment. There were unquestionably positive aspects to this development, in that Christian moral values – especially concerning the care of widows and orphans – were afforded greater cultural influence. But it led to Christianity losing at least something of its prophetic role, as bishops increasingly became political rather than spiritual figureheads.

The rise of the monastic movement partly reflected concern about the direction the Church had been taking, and indicated a longing to escape the complexities and compromises of power. Many monasteries were founded in the deserts of Egypt and often took the form of walled compounds. The walls did more than provide physical security against wild animals and marauders: they were symbols of the community of faith's determination to concentrate on prayer, worship and service, and not to be swamped by the concerns and prevailing ideologies of the world.

For the monks of those orders, withdrawing from the world was the best way of preserving the life of faith. Whether we agree with them or not on this point, we have to concede that the world can easily draw us into its ways of thinking and being. The Church, understood as the 'community of faith' or the 'communion of saints', is about safeguarding the integrity of our faith. It is a place for building our spiritual fitness so we have the energy to work and witness in the world.

There is something of a dilemma for Christians to face here. To serve the world we need to withdraw from it from time to time. If we are to be the 'salt of the earth' and the 'light of the world', we need to preserve our saltiness and keep our batteries charged. Both these helpful images are found in the Sermon on the Mount, in which Jesus says:

> You are the salt of the earth; but if salt has lost its taste, how can its saltiness be restored? It is no longer good for anything, but is thrown out and trampled underfoot. You are the light of the world. A city built on a hill cannot be hid. No one after lighting a lamp puts it under the bushel basket, but on the lampstand, and it gives light to all in the house. In the same way, let your light shine before others, so that they may see your good works and give glory to your Father in heaven.
>
> (Matthew 5.13–16)

Note that these images emphasize the importance of being noticed, whether through taste or sight. But they also express the need to maintain our distinctiveness. Salt can lose its taste; lamps can run out of olive oil. Or, picking up on the image of the Church as a boat, 'the place for the ship is the sea, but God help the ship if the sea gets into it' (D. L. Moody).[7] One of the roles of the Church is to sustain and support us in the life of faith.

In the first volume in this series, *Faith and the Creeds*, we noted how Christianity gives us a distinct way of seeing things. Let's now look at how the Church helps us to develop and sustain this.

The Church as a community of vision

Austin Farrer, an Oxford colleague of C. S. Lewis, once remarked that we 'see through the Church of Christ as a man sees through the telescope to the stars'.[8] It's an interesting idea, especially for a former amateur astronomer like myself! I used to love the cold and crisp winter nights when the night sky could be seen clearly. I knew the names of the constellations, and took great pleasure in following the movement of the planets against the background of the stars.

When I made my first telescope, I discovered that it opened up new riches. I was looking at the same night sky, but now I could make out far more stars than before. I could see the surface of the moon in great detail and the moons of the planet Jupiter. Through the telescope's greater light-gathering power, things that had always been there, but were invisible to the unaided eye, suddenly sprang to sight.

This is one of the points that Farrer is making. A telescope helps us see the stars. The Church – as a community of believers – helps us see ourselves and the world more effectively than would otherwise be the case. Why? Because we pool our spiritual wisdom. We view the Christian faith through other people's eyes, and realize that our own understanding needs to be expanded. We share ways of thinking about core Christian ideas. We listen to other people describing how their faith helps them cope with life's traumas and triumphs, and learn from them. Or we hear people talk about the writers they have read who enabled them to grasp a difficult point or inspired them to serve God in new ways. The Christian Church is a community of learning, which helps us to go deeper and further into our faith.

C. S. Lewis emphasizes this in *Mere Christianity*, as he draws on his own experience of spiritual growth and theological reflection. 'The one really adequate instrument for learning about God is the Christian community, waiting for Him together.'[9] It is within such a community of people 'united together in a body, loving one another, helping one another, showing [God] to one another' that the life of faith takes

root and develops. Although Lewis found his faith stimulated and enriched in other ways – most notably, through
the group of colleagues that we know as 'the Inklings' – there
is no doubting the importance he attached to the local church
as a means of grace.

But Farrer was making another point as well. The Church
helps us develop habits of thinking and acting that are
grounded in the Christian faith – what we might call 'a
discipleship of the mind'. The local church enables us to
grasp the Christian story, and learn to *inhabit* it, not simply
to understand it. The church provides a community that is
nourished by this way of thinking – for instance, through
preaching that illuminates our minds, transforms our hearts
and inspires us to take action. Preaching is theology on fire!
It enables us to make connections between the horizontal
and vertical dimensions of life.

We shall have more to say about the life of faith in the
final volume of this series, *The Christian Life and Hope*. In
the meantime, let's consider briefly the Church as a community that sustains the Christian faith. The sociologist
Peter Berger coined the phrase 'plausibility structures' to refer
to an environment that reinforces a faith. In the seventeenth
century, Western culture was shaped by the presuppositions
of Christian belief, and thus it often promoted some of its
core themes. In the intensely secular culture of the twenty-
first century, the assumptions of faith are challenged if not
actually ridiculed. Christians can easily feel demoralized and
intimidated, tempted to 'go with the flow'. But the Christian
community offers an environment that allows the growth
rather than the withering of faith. This should not in any
way deter us from exploring Christian ideas, or reflecting on
how they may be challenged by a secular culture.

Finally, the Church is a community of moral vision – a group of people who find that their faith leads them to see the world in a new way and act in accordance with that way of seeing. For example, the Christian doctrine of creation reminds us that the world is God's, not ours. We are its stewards, not its owners; it has been entrusted to us, who bear God's image. The new (and welcome) awareness of environmental concerns on the part of so many Christians is grounded in such fundamental theological beliefs. We are to see nature not as something that exists for our convenience but as God's precious possession, entrusted to us for safe-keeping. And once we see nature in that light and in that manner, our behaviour towards it changes.

The word 'church' has been used extensively throughout this chapter, and as there are so many different Christian churches in the world today, some readers may perhaps have been wondering which church we are talking about. Surely we need to clarify what is meant by this word?

Denominations and divisions: which church?

The Christian faith spread rapidly in the Mediterranean area in the first century, with congregations being established in many parts of Asia Minor and Europe, including Rome, the capital city of the Empire. Although these congregations were probably quite small, meeting in houses for fear of the authorities, they appear to have seen themselves as part of a greater community of Christian believers, dispersed throughout the civilized world of the time.

Tensions always existed within the early church – for example, over which bishops took priority within the global Christian community. As the Roman Empire started to fall apart in the fifth century, two quite distinct forms of Christianity began to solidify: the Latin-speaking church of the West, and the Greek-speaking church of the East. Relations between them were bad and eventually became so strained that they ceased seeing themselves as parts of a single church. In 1054, the Great Schism led to the separation of these two bodies, each of which saw itself as the 'true Church'.

Further division took place in the sixteenth century in Western Europe, when the Protestant Reformation led to the fragmentation of the medieval church. Territorial churches – such as the Church of England – emerged, followed by independent groups such as the Baptists. Today, there are tens of thousands of Christian denominations, each regarding itself as either the 'true' Church or, at the very least, as a valid form of the Church. What are we to make of this?

Like many before me, I regard C. S. Lewis's notion of 'mere Christianity' to be helpful in framing our reflections on this question. We touched on this idea in *Faith and the Creeds*, and it's worth exploring further at this point. After his conversion, Lewis felt the need to make a public demonstration of his faith. He wanted to 'show the flag'. As he was an Oxford don at Magdalen College, he decided to start going to college chapel. And he also began attending Holy Trinity Church in Headington, the village just outside Oxford where he lived.[10] He was quite happy (as we saw earlier in this chapter) to describe himself as a 'layman of the Church of England'.

Yet Lewis never saw his identity as a member of the Church of England as implying the supremacy of this denomination. It was his personal choice and, as his later writings make clear, he saw no reason either to regret it or to impose this choice on – or even to recommend it to – anyone else. Why? Because of his idea of 'mere Christianity'.

Lewis borrowed this term from the writings of the Anglican clergyman Richard Baxter (1615–91), who used it to refer to 'Christian basics'. Lewis, like Baxter, disliked denominational politics and wanted to focus on the themes of a basic consensual Christianity, shorn of the specific denominational ideas and practices that so often became the cause of bad-tempered controversy or arrogant assertions of superiority. 'You will not learn from me whether you ought to become an Anglican, a Methodist, a Presbyterian, or a Roman Catholic.'[11] Yet Lewis was clear that being a Christian meant being associated with the community of faith. Christianity was not a solitary religion: it entailed being involved with a church that would provide a wellspring for the development of faith.

Lewis's analogy for explaining the place of denominations in the Christian life has become well known and remains helpful. It enables us to grasp that Lewis is not advocating the abolition of individual Christian denominations or suggesting that these cannot play an important role in living out the Christian faith. What he is proposing is that each denomination should be seen as a distinct version of something more fundamental – 'mere Christianity'.

> [Mere Christianity is] like a hall out of which doors open into several rooms. If I can bring anyone into that hall I shall have done what I attempted. But it is in the rooms, not in the hall, that there are fires and chairs and meals. The hall is a place to wait in, a place from which to try the various doors, not a place to live in.[12]

Let's explore this analogy in more depth.

By using the image of a hall, Lewis prompts us to imagine a large, open space to which all Christians have access. The form of Christianity he has in mind is based on the Bible and the creeds, which focus on the essentials of faith and are generous about how these may be put into practice. Lewis recognizes that Christians do have different views on various things – for example, whether churches should be governed by bishops or congregations, or whether infants should be baptized – and he is aware that some Christians regard these matters as important. However, Lewis suggests we try to see these divergences in their proper perspective, and one way of doing so is to imagine that the large hall leads into smaller rooms. It's important to appreciate that you can reach these smaller rooms in no other way than through the hall, which is a 'common area' for all Christians, while the rooms are where specific kinds of Christians meet.

Lewis is not advocating a 'denominationless Christianity'. He's not saying that Christians should live apart from a community of faith – after all, he himself attended his local church every Sunday with his brother Warren. The essential thing is for Christians to see their commitment to the Christian faith as *primary*, and their allegiance to a specific denomination as *secondary*. That does not mean that denominations are unimportant! It is simply to put them in context so that we realize that they are not of *ultimate* importance.

What then might be the value of different denominations? The answer lies in Lewis's emphasis that the rooms have something that you don't find in the hall – namely, 'fires and chairs and meals'. In 1940s England – when Lewis first delivered the talks eventually published as *Mere Christianity* – these three items turned a house into a home. A cold and lifeless building became a warm and welcoming place in which to live. Denominations offer us a place where we feel we belong. My local church provides our congregation with spiritual warmth, comfort and sustenance.

Which denomination, you might be wondering, is to be preferred? I can't answer that question for you, but I can set it in context. In the next chapter, we shall look at the four 'marks' or 'notes' of the Church. This may be helpful in reflecting on the nature of the Church and its mission, as well as our own denominational identity.

5

One holy catholic and apostolic Church

———•◦•———

The day of Pentecost is often marked as the 'birthday of the Church'. According to the Acts of the Apostles (chapter 2), the climax of the work of the Holy Spirit was to spark into life the Church as a community of believers. The same Spirit, who hovered over the face of the deep in creation and inspired the prophets, initiated the mission of the Church into all the world.

Before Pentecost, there had been gatherings of the original disciples who spent time reflecting on the life, death and resurrection of Jesus of Nazareth. After Pentecost, a new and increasingly diverse group rapidly emerged – believers who had not been disciples but were now convinced of the truth of the gospel. We've already come across the Greek word *ekklēsia* – a gathering or assembly of those who are 'called out' – that came to be used to refer to this new community.

As the Church grew in numbers and influence, it was forced to think through some fundamental questions. What did it believe? How should it worship? What was its relationship with Judaism? Or with paganism? Many of these discussions are echoed in the New Testament itself. One further question had to be explored: what was the Church?

How was this new community of faith to understand its own identity?

The creeds present us with a framework for making sense of that identity, focusing on four key themes. The Nicene Creed declares that Christians believe in 'one holy catholic and apostolic Church'. In this chapter, we shall explore each of these four 'marks' and consider how they help shape our understanding of the nature, mission and purpose of the Church.[1]

We will then look at the role it can play in the Christian life. After all, the Church is something that we inhabit, not something we simply think about!

The first mark: one Church

I used to find it baffling that there were so many churches. In my home town in Ireland, we had churches to meet most tastes – provided, of course, that you were interested in God. I wasn't, and that ruled them all out as far as I was concerned. So many of these churches seemed to have come about as a consequence of disputes that happened generations ago, which nobody had got round to sorting out. So the Nicene Creed's statement that there was 'one Church' seemed totally unrealistic to me. And, to be honest, there are times when it still does. Many times.

However, we can make some sense of this. Let's begin by looking at the New Testament. Paul's letters inform us that individual Christian communities were growing up throughout the civilized world of his era, especially in the great cities of Asia Minor. Paul refers to these communities as 'churches' – that is, as assemblies of people who have been 'called out' of the world. Each of these assemblies had its own distinct identity and – as Paul's letters make clear – its own problems and issues to sort out. Yet it is evident that these individual groups of believers saw themselves as part of something greater that somehow transcended their local communities and their own specific situations. In the later writings of the New Testament, the term 'church' – in the singular – increasingly comes to be used to refer to the body of Christians throughout the world.

The basic assumption is that, since there is only one gospel, there can only be one Church. There is 'one Lord, one faith, one baptism' (Ephesians 4.5). Anyone who responds to this Lord in faith and is baptized is therefore a member of the Church. The Nicene Creed's declaration that there is only one Church thus affirms that there is only one Jesus of Nazareth. The Church is the community of those who put their faith in him. This community is presently dispersed across the world and throughout history; yet, in the end, all its members will be gathered together in the New Jerusalem. There can be only one such community, since there is only one gospel. The second-century theologian Irenaeus of Lyons put it like this:

> The Church having received this preaching and this faith, although scattered throughout the whole world, yet, as if occupying only one house, carefully preserves it. She also believed these points [of faith] just as if she had only one soul, and one and the same heart, and she proclaims them, teaches them, and hands them down with perfect harmony, as if she possessed one mouth.[2]

The letters to the Colossians and Ephesians also emphasize this point of the unity of the Church. Jesus is described as the 'head of the body, the church' (Colossians 1.18). The same term 'church' is thus used to describe both a local gathering of believers and the greater universal reality of all believers. One very simple way of thinking of this relationship is to say that each local church is an embodiment or manifestation of the universal Church, which consists of all believers down the ages.

This might seem to suggest that congregations are to be seen as local branches of banks or supermarkets, and this notion does actually have some relevance! For example, the Church of England is a national church, represented throughout the nation in parish churches, and many other denominations have similar structures. But the New Testament does not advocate an organizational arrangement with a focus on the here and now. It thinks more in terms of the continuity between local Christian gatherings and the entire body of believers – past, present and future – who will one day gather in the New Jerusalem.

An institutional approach to understanding the unity of the Church made sense for the first thousand years of Christian history. During this period, there was one church throughout the Roman Empire, whose dispersed leaders were based in its great cities, especially Rome and Constantinople. By 1054, tensions between Greek- and Latin-speaking churches had become so serious that they went their separate ways, in effect leading to the splitting of the Church into what we would now call Catholicism and Orthodoxy. It was now no longer possible to speak of a single universal Church on earth. The situation became more complex in the sixteenth century, with the emergence of Protestantism. Each church saw itself as the most authentic version of Christianity and asked of the others: are they really churches at all?

These debates continue, and it is not my intention to resolve them. But we can reflect on how to understand the relation between local churches, here and now, and the gathered body of believers in the New Jerusalem. The simplest way of thinking of this is to look on the body of believers on earth as the 'wandering people of God', pilgrims on this earth. Other Christians have made this journey before us, just as others will make it after us. Finally, all will join the throngs gathered in the courts of the New Jerusalem.

John Calvin and others drew a distinction that might be helpful here. On the one hand, we have the 'visible church' – the congregations and gatherings of believers that we see throughout the world. On the other, there is the 'invisible church', which is the community of all believers throughout history, including the saints of the Old Testament, who 'died in faith without having received the promises, but from a distance they saw and greeted them' (Hebrews 11.13).

This sets our own faith in a deeper context. It reminds us that we are part of the pilgrim people of God. Others have made this journey before us. We each individually occupy a tiny slice of history; the Church, however, is deeply rooted in history. We are connected by faith to those who have gone before us, who watch over us and encourage us, as a great 'cloud of witnesses' (Hebrews 12.1). It's something we remember when we read the classics of the Christian faith – such as Augustine's *Confessions* (written in 397–8) or Thomas à Kempis's *Imitation of Christ* (written sometime in about 1425) – or when we visit old churches.

However, many readers will feel that C. S. Lewis's notion of 'mere Christianity' (see pp. 85–8) – with its focus on the here and now and its concern to address the many varieties of Christianity he encountered – makes most sense of the idea of one Church and many denominations.[3] Lewis had no interest in making judgements about which way of living out the Christian faith was the best. His point was that we each have to choose where we find 'fires and chairs and meals' – in other words, the community of faith in which we feel at home, and receive spiritual comfort and nourishment.

From what has been said, it is clear that we can make a lot of sense of the Nicene Creed's declaration that there is only one Church. But what about the idea that this Church is holy?

The second mark: a holy Church

A friend of mine was trying to teach a Sunday school class about holiness. He wanted the group of children (that included his son) to think about what the word meant and how they could explain the idea to their friends and family. 'If someone said that I was holy, what would that mean?' he asked. There was an awkward silence. Eventually, his son put up his hand. 'I guess it would mean they don't know you very well.'

The long history of the Christian churches makes many wary of regarding them as 'holy'. It is hard to take this idea seriously when we hear so many stories of clergy involved in child abuse or financial fraud. And what about the wars of religion? They didn't seem particularly holy. Of course, there are people, such as Mother Teresa of Calcutta, who really have lived holy lives. But that doesn't stop us from feeling that it makes little sense to speak of the Church as a whole in this way.

And it's not just the Church that causes us unease. Paul often addresses his letters to the 'saints'. For example, he opens his letter to the church in the Roman colony of Philippi by addressing 'all the saints in Christ Jesus who are in Philippi' (Philippians 1.1). It immediately becomes clear that he is not referring to some special category of Christians at Philippi, but everyone, including those he believes are behaving badly.

So are all Christians *really* holy? I'm certainly not. Maybe I ought to be, but I'm honest enough to know my many failings. As Groucho Marx's famous one-liner goes: 'I don't want to belong to any club that would have me as a member.'4 Why? Because the admissions standard would have to be ridiculously low! If I'm a saint, the currency has been devalued.

Let's try shifting our thinking from the Church to the idea of 'holiness' itself. For most today, the word suggests stern prohibitions against drinking, dancing and playing cards. Or an austere other-worldly piety, disconnected from the banality of real life. However, these forms of behaviour could be seen as specific cultural implementations of the idea of holiness, which may have made sense in some situations but now seem tired and outdated.

The basic sense of the word 'holy' is 'to be set apart for God' or 'to be dedicated to God'. The call to holiness is of major importance for individual believers and for the Church. 'Be holy, for I am holy' (Leviticus 11.44; 1 Peter 1.16). To be a Christian believer – or a Christian church – is to reflect the character of God. And how do we know what God is like? As we have seen, the classic Christian answer to this question is that God is like Jesus of Nazareth. By becoming more like Jesus, we become more like God.

To be like God is to be faithful, truthful, compassionate and righteous. It means crucifying our old natures, or healing our wounded souls, in order that a new way of living and thinking can emerge. (As we saw earlier, Augustine of Hippo saw the gospel as a healing balm, which restored humanity to what God intended us to be. Perhaps this helps us understand why one of Augustine's favourite ways of thinking about the Church was as a hospital – a place where people came for healing.) But how might this work out in any specific personal or cultural context?

It could help to think of holiness as being less about the way in which we behave and more about the mindset we adopt. Holiness is a principled intention to be Christ-like, expressed in action. Then again, it is not always easy to convert our attitude to specific behaviour! Jesus of Nazareth's summary of the law gives us the guidance we need to begin living a 'holy' life: we are to love God with all our heart, soul, mind and strength, and love our neighbour as ourselves (Matthew 22.34–46). But what might this mean in day-to-day terms?

Some time ago, I read a piece by the American political statesman Henry Kissinger. It was a foreword to the memoirs of Raymond Aron (1905–83), one of the great political philosophers of the twentieth century. Kissinger valued philosophy because it emphasized the importance of truth. But it proved difficult to apply this in practice.

> The philosopher deals with truth; the statesman addresses contingencies. The thinker has a duty to define what is right; the policymaker must deal with what is attainable. The professor focuses on ultimate goals; the diplomat knows that his is a meandering path on which there are few ultimate solutions and whatever 'solutions' there are more often than not turn into a threshold for a new set of problems.[5]

I've often thought that Kissinger's remarks help us reflect on the difficulty of being holy in today's world. The Church has a good sense of what is true, right and our ultimate goal. The real test is to figure out how this might be put into practice in the 'meandering paths' of our lives and our churches.

But there's another challenge that the Church has faced down the centuries as it reflects on the theme of holiness – namely, how to cope with the failings of human nature. Dietrich Bonhoeffer is one of many to have pointed out how Christian communities break down countless times because of an unrealistic view of human nature, leading to disillusionment.[6] How can we be holy, if we're not capable of living up to the expectations we have of ourselves?

This issue regularly surfaces in church life, and there has been much theological reflection on it. Perhaps the most famous debate, which erupted in the early church, was the Donatist controversy. Beginning in the third century, it rumbled on for the next hundred years or so. During the short-lived and ultimately unsuccessful Diocletian persecution of 251, Christian leaders in North Africa were faced with a choice: hand over their Christian books or face death. Many capitulated, unable to cope with the stress. What was to be done with these Christian leaders? A rigorist faction, led by Donatus, held that their failure compromised their integrity. The Church was meant to be holy, so how could it allow such people to remain as leaders? Or even as members of congregations? To maintain the holiness of the Church, it was necessary to be vigilant about church membership and weed out those who failed to live up to their calling.

Another faction, led by Augustine of Hippo, took a different view. Human nature is flawed and weak. We are simply not capable of living up to the full demands of the law, even with the help of God's grace. Failure is the inevitable result of human frailty and sinfulness. Church leaders who lapse under pressure should be readmitted, once they have admitted their failings. It is unrealistic to expect Christians to be perfect in this life. Both church policy and pastoral care need to recognize the limited ability of Christian believers to achieve the holiness to which they are called!

Where does this leave our discussion about the holiness of the Church? We might surmise that holiness can be thought of as a goal, rather than something achievable in the present. It marks the end of our journey, not our present position or condition. The Church is 'holy' in that its individual members are called, inspired and enabled by a holy God, who foresees the end of the transformation that has been begun in our lives.

In *The Living God*, we used another analogy for this process: Michelangelo sculpting his magnificent statue of David from a damaged block of marble. Michelangelo could 'see' the final masterpiece as he worked, and this vision guided and encouraged him. As we look around our churches, we may feel despondent about their leadership and their members. But God sees ahead to what we will finally become. And so must we.

C. S. Lewis made this point beautifully in *The Screwtape Letters*. He points out how those who have just discovered Christianity often have totally unrealistic expectations of what Christians ought to be like. These 'dreaming aspirations' may well get shattered the moment a recent convert starts going to church and sees ordinary people, not saints:

When he goes inside, he sees the local grocer with rather an oily expression on his face bustling up to offer him one shiny little book containing a liturgy which neither of them understands, and one shabby little book containing corrupt texts of a number of religious lyrics, mostly bad, and in very small print. When he gets to his pew and looks round him he sees just that selection of his neighbours whom he has hitherto avoided.[7]

Lewis's description of a 1940s English church rang true with many at the time! His point, though, is timeless. The Church is God's work-in-progress, as God takes ordinary people and makes them extraordinary. We must seek to see the hearts and minds of those who have discovered something precious and vital – a treasure that is contained within (and so often concealed by!) a humble outward appearance.

The third mark: a catholic Church

The third mark of the Church emphasizes its universality. In some versions of the creeds, the phrase 'one holy catholic and apostolic Church' is replaced with 'one holy universal and apostolic Church'. This is a perfectly acceptable translation, although many would feel that it is important to retain the word 'catholic' for historical reasons. In this section, we shall use the term 'catholic' throughout, although you are welcome to replace it with 'universal' if this is helpful.

What does it mean to speak of the 'catholicity' of the Church? And why does it matter? Let's begin by clarifying what the word means. Like so many words that relate to the Christian faith, it is based on a Greek phrase. This phrase, *kath' holou*, means 'relating to the whole' or 'universal'. It came to be used at an early stage in Christian history to refer to the idea that the Church is able to embrace, transform and save men and women of any nation, race or social standing. Early hints of this point can be found in the New Testament, which makes clear that human social evaluations of someone's importance should not carry weight within the Christian community: 'There is no longer Jew or Greek, there is no longer slave or free, there is no longer male and female; for all of you are one in Christ Jesus' (Galatians 3.28).

We know that the early church had to come to terms with a growing body of Christians from diverse backgrounds.[8] Some were Jews who saw Christianity as the fulfilment of their faith. Many were Greeks and Romans, who came to see Christianity as displacing traditional pagan philosophies and religions. The new converts included high-ranking Romans and slaves, men and women. So how was the new movement to cope with this rapid expansion and diversification? Would tensions between different groups lead to the formation of ethnic churches? There are hints in the New Testament, particularly in the Acts of the Apostles, that some would have welcomed such a development. But at an early stage this possibility was rejected. Just as there was only one gospel, so there was only one Church. And that gospel and Church were able to meet the needs of all people groups.

By the middle of the third century, Christian theologians had developed a mature understanding of the catholicity of the Church. In a series of lectures given to those preparing for baptism in the fourth century, Cyril of Jerusalem explained what was meant by this idea:

> The Church is called 'catholic' because it extends through all the world, from one end of the earth to the other; and because it teaches completely, and without any omissions, all the doctrines that ought to be known to humanity concerning both

things that are visible and invisible and things that are earthly
and heavenly; and because it brings all kinds of people –
whether rulers or subjects, learned or ignorant – under the
influence of true piety; and because it universally treats and
cures every kind of sin, whether committed by the soul or
the body; and possesses in itself every kind of virtue which
can be named relating to words, deeds or spiritual gifts of
every kind.[9]

This rich passage sets out four basic ideas. First, the Christian
Church is 'catholic' or 'universal' because it extends throughout the entire world. There is no region in which it is absent.
Wherever there are people, there the Church must be – and
will be. This was one of the motivations driving Christian
mission in Latin America, Africa and Asia.

Second, the Church is universal because 'it teaches completely, and without any omissions,' the whole body of Christian
truth. This is an important point, which we considered in
Faith and the Creeds. The Church is the depository and trans-
mitter of the whole Christian faith, not simply those parts
of it that are thought to be relevant to its own situation.

As someone who has studied the history of the Church, I
have often noticed the tendency of one generation to regard
some aspect of the Christian tradition as being of little interest, only for a later generation to rediscover its importance.
The survival of the Christian faith depends upon the full
richness of its intellectual, spiritual and ethical teachings
being preserved and transmitted. We simply do not know
what challenges we may face in the future, and which of the
many resources of our faith may come into their own in
meeting them. Christianity doesn't always need to develop
new ideas; it can reach back into its past, and rediscover ideas
and approaches that have a new relevance in today's context.

That's one of the big themes that C. S. Lewis develops. Lewis discovered that many classic theological ideas developed by Christian writers of the Renaissance could help him think through the big questions of faith. This naturally made him want to share these with his readers. In works like *Mere Christianity*, Lewis took some classic Christian themes and gave them a new lease of life by reworking them and presenting them in imaginative and creative ways. We see the same pattern time and time again, especially in the field of spirituality. Modern writers discover the rich potential of earlier thinkers and interpret and present them in new and helpful ways, so that they can enrich us today.

My own special interest is the relation of science and faith. Back in the 1990s, I was trying to develop a way of thinking that would provide a good framework for thinking about integrating scientific and Christian ways of thinking about creation. I soon realized that others had thought about these questions long before me! There was no need to reinvent the wheel! In his commentary on the book of Genesis, written around 401, Augustine of Hippo talked about creation as an instantaneous act of God, which brought the universe into being, followed by a long process of development, guided by God's providence. It's a very helpful approach. Yet it's just one example of how earlier Christian thinkers can stimulate and resource us today. Most of the great questions of faith have been discussed by earlier generations, and we can learn by listening in on their conversations. The Church is thus a repository of inherited wisdom, available for us to rediscover and reappropriate.

Third, the Church is there for every kind of person. We might call this a 'sociological catholicity'. To put it technically, we could say that the Christian faith transcends human social constructions, such as nationality or class. The Church declares that there is a vertical dimension to our life that is, in the end, more important than any of its horizontal dimensions. This does not mean that Christianity devalues or denies things that really matter to people, such as their nationality or ethnic identity. It simply asks us to avoid thinking that these are of ultimate importance.

In practice, Christianity affirms the importance of the universality of the Church, while respecting particularities. Churches frequently develop specialist ministries, often because particular groups are seen to have special needs. Individual congregations can develop a social identity, mirroring the locality in which they are based. But the basic point remains the same: the Church is, and is meant to be, for all who are drawn to God.

Finally, the Church is entrusted with a gospel that is able to meet the needs of all people. It 'universally treats and cures every kind of sin'. The Church has the resources to deal with the problems of humanity – past, present and future. But that doesn't mean that the Church can be complacent. Each generation has to ensure that the Christian faith is explained and communicated effectively, rather than relying on what previous generations found accessible and helpful. Why is this important? Well, one of the points that I take away from reflecting on this section of the creed is summed up in Cyril of Jerusalem's remark that the Church is called to teach 'completely, and without any omissions, all the doctrines which ought to be known'. I find this challenging because I have settled into my own way of thinking about the Christian faith, which highlights some of its themes and tends to overlook or marginalize some others. Now I'm not alone in doing this! But it's not right.

The creeds challenge us not to become complacent or lazy. They offer us a map, so that we can explore the landscape of faith more fully. If some theme seems unimportant or uninteresting to us, maybe it's because we haven't investigated it properly. This is an especially important point for preachers, who all too often orbit their own particular favourite topics and texts and fail to encourage and enable their congregations to discover the full riches of faith.

The fourth mark: an apostolic Church

Finally, we turn to consider what it signifies to say that the Church is 'apostolic'. The word 'apostle' is derived from the Greek verb *apostellein*, 'to send out', and means something like a 'messenger' or 'emissary'. In the New Testament, it has the developed sense of 'someone who is commissioned to preach the good news' or 'someone who Jesus of Nazareth authorized to preach on his behalf'. The Gospels speak of Jesus singling out twelve of his disciples and naming them 'apostles' (Mark 3.14; Luke 6.13), and there are occasional references to this inner group of disciples as 'the Twelve' (Matthew 10.2).

In the New Testament letters, the word is used in a slightly different sense, meaning those who have been indirectly commissioned by Jesus of Nazareth to proclaim the good news. Perhaps the most obvious example is Paul of Tarsus, who clearly understood that he had encountered the risen Christ on the road to Damascus and been commanded to preach in his name. Paul's major letters to the churches at Rome and Corinth all open with a declaration of his calling to be an apostle. Other figures in the New Testament, including Barnabas and Apollos, are also referred to in this way. At one point, there is a suggestion that this role became part of the ministry of the churches – for example, the letter to the Ephesians speaks of some within the churches being called to be 'apostles, some prophets, some evangelists, some pastors and teachers' (Ephesians 4.11).

What does it mean to speak of the Church as 'apostolic'? For many Christians, the idea of 'apostolic succession' is important, as it highlights the continuity between the churches of today and the first Christian community. There are three basic points to explore.

The first is historical. The Church can track its origins back to the apostles. This was of huge importance to the early church, as it faced off rival visions of Christianity that emerged in the second century. These had no connection with the apostles and were often recent inventions of maverick writers who mimicked the style of the Gospels or argued that they had some special divine endorsement (not recognized by anyone else, of course) to preach a new gospel.

The early Christian writer Irenaeus of Lyons (*c.* 130–*c.* 200) emphasized that the Church had inherited two things from the apostles: the texts that we now call the New Testament, and the right way of interpreting these texts. Historical continuity with the apostles was seen as safeguarding the apostolic preaching. The Church taught what they taught, having 'received this tradition from the apostles'.[10]

The second theme emphasizes this further: the first Christians are recorded as having 'devoted themselves to the apostles' teaching' (Acts 2.42). In one of his earliest letters, Paul asked believers to 'stand firm and hold fast to the traditions' that they had been taught by himself, Silvanus and Timothy (2 Thessalonians 2.15). The later letters continue to emphasize the importance of receiving and passing on the apostolic teaching, which is described as the 'good treasure entrusted to you' (2 Timothy 1.14).

Two complementary, yet distinct, models of ensuring connection with the apostolic church have developed within Christianity. The first holds that links with the apostles are best maintained and demonstrated institutionally: that is, through bishops who can demonstrate a continuity of succession back through history, eventually connecting up with the apostles themselves. The second places an emphasis upon the Bible as a record of the apostolic teaching, and holds that continuity with the 'good treasure entrusted to you' is maintained through the public reading of the Bible at Christian worship and through preaching on its themes.

The third point concerns the Church continuing the evangelistic, pastoral and social ministry of the apostles. Many churches follow a three-fold understanding of this ministry, consisting of bishops, presbyters or priests, and deacons. Today's ministers continue with the ministry of the apostles – for example, in baptizing people, or in inviting believers to share in bread and wine, following Jesus' command to his disciples to do this in remembrance of him (Luke 22.19).

Taken together, these three aspects of the apostolicity of the Church speak to us of a community that is deeply rooted in history, concerned to safeguard and pass on its good news for the world. Yet the idea of the apostolicity of the Church also speaks to each believer in a much deeper way. It reassures us that we are connected by faith to the apostles themselves. They are part of our history; we are part of theirs.

There is much more that could be said about each of these four 'marks' of the Church, although some readers may feel that our discussion has already gone far beyond the theme of 'the Spirit of grace'! But the Church was called into being by that Spirit, which continues to guide and energize it, so we cannot avoid thinking about its shape, form and function. The creeds provide us with a toolkit for deepening our understanding of the nature of the Church, so we can build this into our thinking.

In bringing our reflections on the Church to a close, let's reflect on an analogy for the Christian community that many within today's Western cultural context find especially helpful: the idea of the Church as a 'colony of heaven'.

The Church as a colony of heaven

The letters of the New Testament were written at a time when Roman power was at its greatest. Rome established and maintained its authority by means of the colony (Latin: *colonia*). In one of his letters, Paul develops the idea of the Church as a 'colony' – not of Rome, but of heaven. What might he have meant by this?

Unfortunately, modern Western ideas of 'colonies' are largely shaped by the outcome of European imperialism in the nineteenth century, when overseas territories were in effect annexed as belonging to a European state, such as Great Britain or France. The Roman idea of a colony was very different. For a start, the term referred, not to a territory, but to a city or township. When a city was conquered, its administration was handed over to Roman settlers. Typically, a city would be populated by Roman citizens or by inhabitants of the region around Rome ('Latins'). These colonies would be seen as extensions of the mother city abroad, with citizens enjoying the right of return to Rome.

Rome, of course, was not alone in establishing colonies in the ancient world. Many Greek cities established colonies, and one such was Krenides in Macedonia. This city was captured by Philip, the father of Alexander the Great, and renamed Philippi in his honour. It was taken over by the Romans in 148 BC, and in New Testament times was populated by Roman citizens and governed according to Roman law.[11] Although Philippi was situated in the Greek-speaking Roman province of Macedonia, its official language was Latin and its public buildings were modelled on those of Rome. Philippi was, in effect, a relocated, scaled-down version of that great city.

This historical detail is needed to make sense of one of the most remarkable features of Paul's letter to the church at Philippi: its use of the Roman *colonia* as a way of understanding the place of the Church. Paul assumes that his readers in Philippi, already familiar with this political model, will understand his allusion to the situation in the colony and its implications for thinking about the Christian life. 'Our citizenship is in heaven, and it is from there that we are expecting a Saviour, the Lord Jesus Christ' (Philippians 3.20).[12] What does he mean?

The immediacy of Paul's analogy is now lost on us, and we must therefore reconstruct and analyse what would have been intuitive and obvious to Paul's original intended readers. The best sermon analogies are fresh and imaginatively compelling, making immediate and plausible connections with the life and experience of their audience. Two thousand years later, this one needs exploring and unpacking.

Paul's central theme is that, just as Philippi saw itself as an outpost of Rome in the distant province of Macedonia, so Christians must see themselves as a colony of heaven on earth. The idea of Christians being 'citizens of heaven' came naturally to Paul, since he himself held Roman citizenship and was aware of the privileges that this brought. There are three ways in which Paul's analogy would have connected with his readers in Philippi.

First, Philippi was not where they really belonged. They were Romans. Roman citizens residing in Philippi had the right to return home to the metropolis after their service in the colony. Paul's point is that one of the 'benefits of Christ' – that is, what Jesus of Nazareth won for believers by his obedience, death and resurrection – was the privilege of being a citizen of heaven. The greatest privilege of a citizen of a great city was the right to live there permanently. Roman citizens had the right to reside in the world's greatest city, even though they might serve the Empire in some of its most far-flung regions.

Second, the Roman colony at Philippi spoke Latin, the language of their native Rome. The practicalities of living in Macedonia required that they be able to speak other languages (Paul, after all, wrote in Greek to the church at Philippi). Nevertheless, they kept their native language alive. And third, they observed the laws and customs of Rome at Philippi. In both these ways – through language and laws – they maintained their identity as Roman citizens. One day they would return to their homeland. In the meantime, they kept alive its memory – partly to recall the past, and partly to anticipate the future.

The Church is a community of believers, a colony of heaven on earth, a place in which the 'Spirit of grace' (Zechariah 12.10, AV) dwells. In its worship and prayer, the Church speaks the language of heaven. Although we live on earth, we observe the customs and values of our real homeland. Christians thus live in two worlds and must learn to negotiate their boundaries.

Moving on

In this book, we have reflected on Christian understandings of the Holy Spirit, human nature and the Church, picking up on some of the statements set out in the Apostles' Creed and the Nicene Creed. We shall have more to say about the place of the Church in Christian life and thought in the next volume in this series, especially as we explore the place of the sacraments in sustaining and informing the life of faith.

Our thoughts now turn to the great theme of the Christian hope and the way in which this transforms and sustains the Christian life. What is this Christian hope and how does it affect how we think and act? In *The Christian Life and Hope*, the final volume in this series, we shall reflect on how the creeds give us a framework for Christian living, as much as for Christian believing.

Notes

Preface

1 William Temple, opening speech at the Second World Conference on Faith and Order, Edinburgh, 1937.

1 The Holy Spirit: the giver of life

1 For the story, see Catherine M. Lewis, *'Don't Ask What I Shot': How Eisenhower's love of golf helped shape 1950s America*. New York: McGraw-Hill, 2007, 63.

2 C. S. Lewis, 'The Grand Miracle,' in *C. S. Lewis: Essay Collection*. London: Collins, 2000, 3–9.

3 This is the Western version of the Nicene Creed, which came into general use in the Latin-speaking Western church in about the year 1000. The original version of the creed, still widely used in Eastern Orthodox churches, speaks of the Spirit proceeding from the Father, not the Father and the Son.

4 Dorothy L. Sayers, *Unpopular Opinions*. London: Victor Gollancz, 1946, 19.

5 John Calvin, *Institutes of the Christian Religion*, III.ii.7.

6 I have used the English translation of Richard F. Littledale (1833–90); the original Italian wording is slightly different.

7 Augustine of Hippo, *Confessions*, I.1.1.

8 C. S. Lewis, *Mere Christianity*. London: HarperCollins, 2002, 172–8.

9 Lewis, *Mere Christianity*, 176–7.

10 Charles Wesley, 'Free grace', stanza 5. This hymn is better known today as 'And can it be?' The stanza I have quoted is rarely sung today.

11 *The Letters of Dorothy L. Sayers, Volume Three.* Cambridge: Dorothy L. Sayers Society, 1998, 255.

12 *Catechism of the Catholic Church*, §737.

2 Humanity: the climax of God's Creation

1 Dorothy L. Sayers, *Unpopular Opinions.* London: Victor Gollancz, 1946, 18.

2 Michael J. Sandel, *Justice: What's the right thing to do?* New York: Farrar, Straus and Giroux, 2009.

3 Francis Crick, *The Astonishing Hypothesis: The scientific search for the soul.* London: Simon & Schuster, 1994, 3.

4 For a discussion of Dawkins' views, see Alister E. McGrath, *Dawkins' God: From the selfish gene to the God delusion.* Second edn. Oxford: Wiley-Blackwell, 2015.

5 See, for example, the analysis in Alister E. McGrath, *The Intellectual Origins of the European Reformation.* Second edn. Oxford: Blackwell, 2003, 34–43; Charles G. Nauert, *Humanism and the Culture of Renaissance Europe.* Cambridge: Cambridge University Press, 2006.

6 Francis Quarles, *Emblems.* London: Hogg, 1778, 202.

7 See further Hans W. Wolff, *Anthropology of the Old Testament.* Philadelphia: Fortress Press, 1974. On early Christian approaches, see M. C. Steenberg, *Of God and Man: Theology as anthropology from Irenaeus to Athanasius.* London: T. & T. Clark, 2009.

8 Julian Ashbourn, *Biometrics: Advanced identity verification.* London: Springer, 2000.

9 Note the points made in Alister McGrath, 'Does religion poison everything? The New Atheism and religious belief', in *Mere Theology: Christian faith and the discipleship of the mind.* London: SPCK, 2010, 119–38.

10 Norman Angell, *The Great Illusion: A study of the relation of military power in nations to their economic and social advantage.* New York and London: G. P. Putnam's Sons, 1910. Angell won the Nobel Peace Prize in 1933.

11 J. R. R. Tolkien, *Tree and Leaf.* London: Harper Collins, 1992, 89.

12 J. C. Ryle, *Expository Thoughts on the Gospels: St Matthew.* Cambridge: James Clarke, 1974, 378.

3 Grace: the gift of a courteous God

1 *Catechism of the Catholic Church*, §1996.

2 Everett Ferguson, *Backgrounds of Early Christianity.* Third edn. Grand Rapids, Michigan: Eerdmans, 2003, 65–6.

3 Ambrose, *De officiis ministrorum*, ii, 28.

4 Alister E. McGrath, *Thomas F. Torrance: An intellectual biography.* Edinburgh: T. & T. Clark, 1999.

5 Thomas F. Torrance, *The Christian Doctrine of God: One being, three persons.* Edinburgh: T. & T. Clark, 1996, 244.

6 See my early work, Alister E. McGrath, *Luther's Theology of the Cross: Martin Luther's theological breakthrough.* Oxford: Blackwell, 1985. A second edition appeared in 2006.

7 See Isaiah Berlin, *The Proper Study of Mankind.* New York: Farrar, Straus, Giroux, 1997; B. W. Young, *Religion and Enlightenment in Eighteenth-Century England: Theological debate from Locke to Burke.* Oxford: Clarendon Press, 1998; Louis Dupré, *The Enlightenment and the Intellectual Foundations of Modern Culture.* New Haven, Connecticut: Yale University Press, 2004.

8 Friedrich Wilhelm Nietzche, *The Anti-Christ*, 1888.

9 Augustine, *Expositions of Psalms 99–120*, iii, 19.

4 The Church: the communion of saints

1 See further Avery Dulles, *Models of the Church.* New York: Doubleday, 2002.

2 John Bowlby, *Maternal Care and Mental Health.* Geneva: World Health Organization, 1952. For a mature statement of the idea of a 'secure base' see John Bowlby, *A Secure Base: Parent–child attachment and healthy human development.* New York: Basic Books, 1988.

3 Cyprian of Carthage, *On the Unity of the Catholic Church*, 6.

4 John Calvin, *Institutes of the Christian Religion*, IV.i.1.

5 Dietrich Bonhoeffer, *Life Together*. London: SCM Press, 1954, 65.

6 C. H. Spurgeon, Sermon 139, preached on 5 July 1857 at the Music Hall, Royal Surrey Gardens, London. The emphasis is in the original.

7 Cited in Gary Inrig, *Hearts of Iron, Feet of Clay*. Chicago: Moody Press, 1979, 11.

8 Cited in Austin Farrer, *The End of Man*. London: SPCK, 1973, 52.

9 C. S. Lewis, *Mere Christianity*. London: HarperCollins, 2002, 165.

10 Headington later became part of the city of Oxford. For details of these developments, see Alister McGrath, *C. S. Lewis – A Life: Eccentric genius, reluctant prophet*. London: Hodder & Stoughton, 2013.

11 Lewis, *Mere Christianity*, viii.

12 Lewis, *Mere Christianity*, 11–12.

5 One holy catholic and apostolic Church

1 For a full discussion, see Alister E. McGrath, *Christian Theology: An introduction*. Oxford: Wiley-Blackwell, 2011, 375–99.

2 Irenaeus of Lyons, *Against All Heresies*, I.x.2.

3 For further discussion, see Alister E. McGrath, 'A "mere Christian": Anglicanism and Lewis's religious identity', in *The Intellectual World of C. S. Lewis*. Oxford: Wiley-Blackwell, 2013, 147–61.

4 There are at least four variants of this quote. I have taken this from Arthur Marx, *My Life with Groucho: A son's eye view*. London: Robson Books, 1988, 187–8.

5 Raymond Aron, *Memoirs: Fifty years of political reflection*. New York: Holmes & Meier, 1990, xi.

6 Dietrich Bonhoeffer, *Life Together*. London: SCM Press, 1954, 15–16.

7 C. S. Lewis, *The Screwtape Letters*. London: HarperCollins, 2002, 5. Lewis is almost certainly basing this on his own experience

at Holy Trinity Church, Headington Quarry, Oxford, which he began to attend in 1930.

8 See Judith Lieu, *Christian Identity in the Jewish and Graeco-Roman World*. Oxford: Oxford University Press, 2004.

9 Cyril of Jerusalem, *Catechetical Lectures*, XVIII, 23.

10 Irenaeus of Lyons, *Against All Heresies*, II.ix.1.

11 For details, see G. Walter Hansen, *The Letter to the Philippians*. Grand Rapids, Michigan: Eerdmans, 2009, 1–6.

12 For detailed comment, see Hansen, *Letter to the Philippians*, 267–77.